CATS

BEHAVIOR • BREEDS • HEALTH • GROOMING

CATS

BEHAVIOR • BREEDS • HEALTH • GROOMING

WELDON
OWEN

Published by Weldon Owen Pty Ltd
59–61 Victoria Street, McMahons Point
Sydney, NSW 2060, Australia
Copyright © 2011 Weldon Owen Pty Ltd

Managing Director Kay Scarlett
Publisher Corinne Roberts
Creative Director Sue Burk
Images Manager Trucie Henderson
Senior Vice President, International Sales Stuart Laurence
Sales Manager, North America Ellen Towell
Administration Manager, International Sales Kristine Ravn
Production Director Todd Rechner
Production and Prepress Controller Mike Crowton
Production Controller Lisa Conway
Production Coordinator Nathan Grice

Designer Jacqueline Richards
Editor Kate McAllan
Editorial Assistant Natalie Ryan

ISBN: 978-1-78342-051-3

Printed by 1010 Printing
Manufactured in China

The paper used in the manufacture of this book is sourced
from wood grown in sustainable forests. It complies with the
Environmental Management System Standard ISO 14001:2004

A WELDON OWEN PRODUCTION

CONTENTS

THE CAT'S WORLD

THE CAT FAMILY

DOMESTIC CATS HAVE shared our lives for some 4,000 years. Although they are loving, affectionate companions, they retain the instinct to hunt, displaying all the skill of their wild relatives—the skill that has made cats one of the most successful mammals of all.

Like many of their fellow cats, the medium-sized lynx mostly hunts at night and rests during the day.

11

IN THE PAST

Lions are perhaps the best known of the 36 species in the cat family.

The carnivorous cat family can trace its history back 35 million years. There are 36 living cat species, from the 600-pound (270 kg) tiger to the 2.5-pound (1 kg) black-footed cat.

CLASS	Mammalia
ORDER	Carnivora
FAMILY	Felidae
SUBFAMILIES	Felinae
	Pantherinae
GENERA	18
SPECIES	36

Modern species of cats share many physical and genetic similarities because they are all descended from a single ancestral species that was similar to an ocelot. This creature lived in Eurasia between 10 and 15 million years ago. From this ancestor, cats diversified and spread, leaving only Australia and Antarctica without native cats. Where several species compete for food in an area, they seem to work things out by hunting at different times of day or pursuing different types of prey.

Big cats, such as this dark leopard, can bring down large mammals.

Small cats, such as the domestic cat, hunt small prey, including rodents and birds.

CATS IN THE WILD

A mountain lion reveals its long canine teeth in a display of threat.

Among the carnivores, cats are perhaps the most impressively adapted for a predatory lifestyle. They are streamlined runners or stealthy ambush hunters, with razor claws and lethal teeth.

A cheetah stretches, showing its long, flexible spine, which helps make it a superb sprinter.

Cats have adapted to a wide range of habitats. This lynx is at home in cold alpine environments.

Recent molecular analyses reveal that modern cats evolved in three distinct lines. The pantherine line is the largest with 24 of the 36 species of living cats. It includes golden cats, servals, pumas, lynxes, cheetahs and all big cats. Another line led to the seven species of small South American cats and a third line to the other species, including the domestic cat and its close relatives. For all their diversity of color, size and habits, the cats are remarkably uniform in body and skull shape, general proportions and especially in their dentition— their long canine teeth are typical of meat eaters.

BIG CATS
Lion

Lions once roamed wide areas of central southern Europe, India and northern Africa. They are now found only in western India, and semidesert and upland areas of Africa.

Among the largest and most powerful of the cat family, lions are the only cats that regularly hunt together and share the spoils. They live in prides, the females of which are usually related. Usually about 12–15 animals live and hunt together in a territory that is patrolled by the dominant males. Young males, pushed out of their family group when their father loses control of it, may form small groups for mutual protection until they can establish themselves in a pride.

The distinctive mane of the male lion is thought to give him protection. A full mane also indicates a healthy, strong animal.

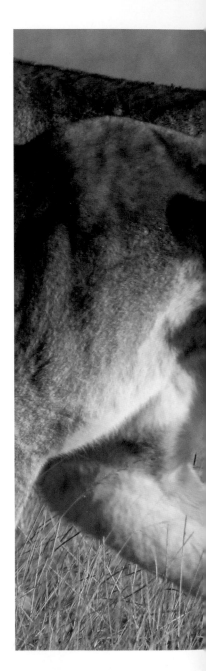

Lionesses live cooperatively, hunting together and even suckling each other's cubs.

BIG CATS
Tiger

There are five subspecies of tiger. They live in a variety of habitats in eastern and southern Asia, from the snow-clad taiga to tropical forests.

A formidable predator, the tiger is the largest of today's cats and the only one with a striped coat. The dark stripes provide camouflage in the low-light conditions in which it hunts, often between dusk and dawn. Tigers are solitary and territorial. Neighboring females have territories that are exclusive or overlapping, while a male's home range may take in that of several breeding females. Litters of two or three cubs are suckled by the mother for about six months, but they remain with her, learning the skills of hunting and survival, until they are about two years old.

Tigers are capable swimmers and sometimes bring down prey in water.

Like all cats, tigers stalk and pounce. Fast and powerful, they bring down large prey such as deer.

The Siberian tiger is the largest of the species. It has a thick coat for protection from the cold.

BIG CATS
Jaguar • Leopard • Snow Leopard

The smaller of the big cats are good climbers and, although they usually hunt on the ground, they often climb into trees and onto rock ledges to rest.

JAGUAR

Jaguars live in swamplands and by forest streams in Central and South America, and are strong swimmers. Their short fur is patterned with dark rosettes. Some animals are entirely black. They are at risk due to the destruction of their habitat.

LEOPARD

Leopards live across much of Africa and Asia, sometimes hunting close to human populations. Their fur varies from gray to rusty brown. Desert and savanna populations are generally paler. They have small black spots and rosettes. All-black leopards are common, especially in tropical forests.

SNOW LEOPARD

Snow leopards live in mountainous areas of central Asia. They have gray-green eyes and long, thick, gray fur with dark spots. The legs are comparatively short, with large, broad paws. They are accomplished at climbing rocky crags.

The snow leopard's lighter colored coat allows it to blend with the snow.

Leopards are capable climbers. They sometimes drag their prey into trees.

Jaguars hunt medium-sized prey. Many are eradicated near ranches.

The Eurasian lynx can be plain or have spots or stripes.

BIG CATS
Puma • Cheetah • Lynx

Although these cats are sometimes included with the "big" cats because they are large, none of them has the ability to roar like the members of the genus *Panthera*.

The Eurasian lynx can be plain or have spots or stripes.

Pumas, also known as mountain lions, are born in litters of up to three.

PUMA

Puma cubs are born with a spotted coat but the spots fade as they mature. The adult's plain coat can be from red-brown to blue-gray. They live in North, Central and South America. There are usually two or three cubs in a litter. They are fully grown and independent at about two years. Adults are basically solitary animals.

CHEETAH

The cheetah is the world's fastest land mammal. It can run at more than 60 miles per hour (100 km/h). It has long powerful legs and a long tail, probably to aid balance. Their claws don't fully retract, giving added traction for maneuvering.

LYNX

All five species in this genus have prominent ears tipped with tufts of black hair. The bobcat has been the most successful in adapting to changing habitat conditions. They hunt small animals such as birds, rabbits and snakes.

The cheetah is slender and long-legged. It is a natural sprinter.

SMALL CATS
Ocelot • Oncilla • Margay

Similar in appearance, these three American cats are all nocturnal. They prey on small animals, such as rodents, insects, birds and reptiles.

The oncilla inhabits mountainous forests.

OCELOT

Ocelots have short fur with spots that sometimes run in lines along the body. Once hunted for its fur and still threatened by forest clearing, its numbers have been greatly reduced.

ONCILLA

The oncilla has thick, soft fur marked with dark spots and rosettes, ideal camouflage for its rain forest habitat. Rare in most of its range, its habitat is shrinking due to logging to make way for coffee plantations.

MARGAY

The margay has soft, thick fur marked with dark streaks or spots. It is usually found in humid tropical forests from Mexico through Central and South America east of the Andes to Argentina.

An agile climber, the margay frequently descends tree trunks head-first.

Ocelots hunt a wide range of prey, from rodents to young deer.

SMALL CATS
Kodkod • Jaguarundi • Andean Mountain Cat

These three small South American cats are surviving with varying success. The jaguarundi is at a low risk but the kodkod and the Andean mountain cat are decreasing in number.

KODKOD

The smallest cat in the Americas is marked with small spots or is completely black. It lives in the forests of the Andes Mountains in a restricted area of Chile and Argentina, and is under threat from logging and agricultural expansion.

JAGUARUNDI

With its flattened head, slender body and short legs, this unspotted cat looks like a weasel or otter. It lives in a variety of habitats from arid thorn forests to dense forests and swampy grasslands. It catches fish and other small prey.

ANDEAN MOUNTAIN CAT

This cat lives in the arid zones of the Andes Mountains. Its thick coat enables it to survive bitterly cold nights. It mainly hunts rodents, including the endangered chinchillas.

The kodkod hunts and rests in trees but also hunts on the ground.

Jaguarundi kittens are born with spots. These soon fade to a plain coat.

Due to its small range, the silvery Andean mountain cat is extremely rare.

SMALL CATS
Asiatic Golden Cat • Pallas Cat • Clouded Leopard

These three Asian cats live in a wide range of habitats, from mountainous regions to deserts, steppes and tropical rain forest.

Clouded leopards prey on birds, monkeys and squirrels in trees and small ground animals.

ASIATIC GOLDEN CAT

This cat's range is from Nepal to south China and Indonesia. It feeds on small and medium-sized mammals, such as rabbits and goats.

PALLAS CAT

This rare cat has short, stout legs. Its dense, long fur provides insulation against the cold, snowy winters that are common throughout most of its range in the steppes of central Asia.

The Asiatic golden cat is unusual among cats as the male helps to raise the kittens.

CLOUDED LEOPARD

This leopard has large cloud-shaped markings. Rarely seen in the wild, it is thought to ambush its prey from trees. It is found in the Himalayas, south China, Taiwan, Malaysia, Sumatra and Borneo.

The Pallas cat is about the same size as a domestic cat. It feeds on small mammals.

SMALL CATS
African Golden Cat • Serval

These two African cats are about the same size, growing to about 39 inches (100 cm), although the serval lives in well-watered grasslands and the golden cat prefers forests.

The serval pounces on its prey and also grabs birds from the air. It can leap over 3 feet (1 m) vertically.

The elusive African golden cat is thought to hunt mostly at dawn and dusk.

AFRICAN GOLDEN CAT

This cat inhabits the equatorial jungles of Senegal, Kenya and northern Angola. It tends to live on the ground and creates its lair under rocks or in holes dug by other animals.

SERVAL

This tall, long-legged cat has a short tail and a small, slim head with large ears. It is tawny gold marked with black dots. Serval mothers give birth to from one to three kittens in a well-camouflaged den or an abandoned burrow dug by another animal. It is found widely throughout Africa and is abundant in areas south of the Sahara.

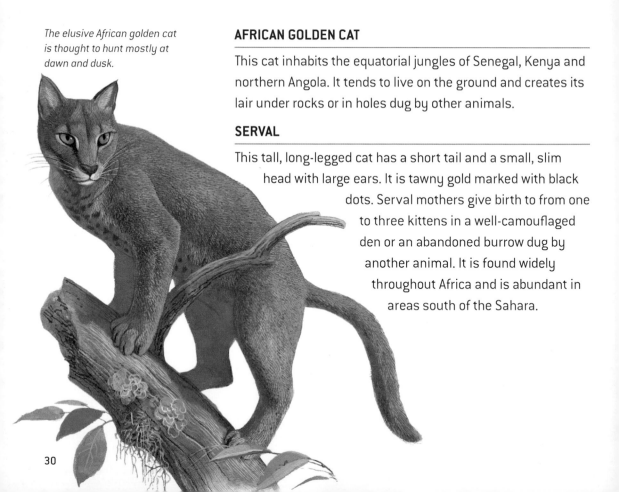

FERAL AND WILD CATS

Feral cats are often aggressive when approached as they are not used to close contact with people.

The wild cat was probably domesticated in Egypt about 4,000 years ago but when domestic cats go feral, their behavior is nothing like that of your mild-mannered pet.

Lost or abandoned domestic cats can quickly become feral, even in the urban environment. They may become so wary of people that they are difficult to reclaim. Feral cats are well able to survive but their predations wreak havoc on local populations of small native animals and birds. They can bear several litters a year and, not being socialized with people early in life, the young grow into adults that are virtually impossible to catch and handle. Their illnesses go untreated and these cats carry parasites and infectious diseases. Fighting is prevalent and infections are quickly passed on.

Wild cats lived in Scotland long before people arrived. The Scottish wild cat is critically endangerd.

In urban environments, stray cats find food and shelter and can quickly breed to large populations.

BIOLOGY AND BEHAVIOR

CATS MAY HAVE BEEN domesticated for thousands of years, but the domestic cat is only a step away from its wild relatives. Its anatomy, instincts and behavioral traits are still uniquely catlike. Coming to terms with this can help us understand their sometimes mystifying behavior.

Cats and dogs are notorious for their hostility. If introduced when young, however, they can get along.

A CAT'S SKELETON

Cats are hunters. Most are solitary predators that stalk their prey then attack in a brief rush. Their anatomical features have evolved to make them superb at this task.

The cat's skeleton comprises some 250 bones. All cat skeletons display variations on a similar theme. Generally, only the relative proportions of various parts vary between cat species, influenced by diet or the cat's living environment. The vertebral column of cats supports the body and allows flexible movement because of its intricate sections. Cats' strong limbs give them a powerful ability to pounce. A cat's trunk is like a taut bow. The muscles of the back and belly provide the tension that allows the body to stretch and contract like a spring, giving it power, speed and flexibility.

This cougar skull shows its typical cat canine teeth, essential for seizing its prey.

Cats have around 40 more bones than humans, mainly in their long tail.

TEETH AND CLAWS

Cats have highly specialized teeth and claws that are adapted to their hunting behavior and diet. They share these adaptations with their wild relatives.

A yawning cat reveals its canines. Kittens are born with 26 teeth and adults have thirty.

STABBING AND CUTTING TEETH

Cats typically have 30 teeth. On each side there are three upper and three lower incisors, an upper and lower canine, three upper and two lower premolars, and an upper and lower molar. The long, rounded canines stab between the neck vertebrae of a cat's prey. Sharp-edged premolars allow the teeth to shear through meat and bone.

When a cat walks, its retracted claws are sheathed, so they remain sharp for use.

CLAW ADVANTAGE

Each digit in a cat's foot has a curved, hollow claw sheathed by skin. When a cat is relaxed, its claws are retracted inside the sheath. When a cat uses its claws, the muscles contract and the claws protrude beyond their sheaths, making formidable fighting and hunting weapons.

LONG AND SHORT HAIR

Hair provides not only insulation but also physical protection for the skin. Most wild cats have short hair, even if the texture varies greatly between the species.

As a result of cross-breeding, the domestic cat comes in a huge variety of hair lengths and types, from the almost hairless Sphynx, to the Persian, with its thick and flowing coat. Normally a cat's coat has three types of hairs—the guard, awn

The Abyssinian is known for its short, fine, shiny coat.

and down. When the guard, the normal dominant hair type, is bred out, as in the Cornish Rex, the result is a soft, wavy coat. Some Persians have extra-long guards, which produces a long, silky coat. In others, the down hairs are as long as the guard hairs, doubling the thickness of the coat.

The coat of the Cornish Rex is completely free of guard hairs, making it short and silky.

Some Persians have extra-long guard hairs and others have down hairs.

COLORS GALORE

Cats in the wild are color adapted and patterned for camouflage. Some natural variation in color occurs. Domestic cats come in a wider range of colors.

The Russian Blue is a uniform blue with a glossy, silver sheen.

The stripes of the tabby pattern come in many color varieties.

Wild species of cat usually have coats that are a mixture of bands or spots. In the wild, color gene mutations occur, particularly black, as seen in leopards. It is likely that black was the first true color mutation for domestic cats as well, probably followed by red and white. These basic colors became the foundation for the myriad colors and patterns that exist today. The names given to the color of a cat's coat differ around the world. Black is often known as ebony. Chocolate Oriental Shorthairs are called Havana in Britain and Chestnut in North America.

While most jaguars are patterned in shades of brown, a few are black.

The Siamese has a cream body with dark highlights on the extremities.

COAT PATTERNS

The tabby pattern clearly comes through on this gray Maine Coon.

The enormous variety of coat patterns and shades among domestic cats are all based on the tabby pattern of their wild ancestor, a pattern that afforded good camouflage.

Selective breeding has brought many different types of spots, tips and pointed patterns. There are four basic types of tabby pattern. Classic tabbies typically have wide stripes with swirls on their flanks centered around a blotch. Mackerel tabby stripes are narrow, parallel, and run from the spine down the flanks to the belly. Spotted tabbies have spots, not stripes. Ticked tabbies have light-colored hairs scattered among dark ones. The patched or mottled tortoiseshell pattern looks somewhat like the patterns seen on the shells of tortoises. The torbie, or patched tabby, is a combination of the tortoiseshell and tabby.

Although coat patterns are all variations on a theme, each cat is unique.

Tortoiseshell coats can come in a range of color combinations.

HEADS AND EARS

Because of selective breeding, the size and shape of a cat's head, as well as the form and placement of its ears, differ widely from breed to breed.

Persian cats have small, rounded ears and a flattened face.

HEAD

The shape of the domestic cat's head can be divided into three basic types. Breeds such as the Siamese and Oriental Shorthair have wedge-shaped or triangular heads. A round head is found in breeds such as the Persian and Exotic Shorthair. The Havana Brown has a rectangular head, broad across the eyes and tapering to a narrower muzzle.

The Scottish Fold is named for its characteristic ears, which fold forward and downward.

EARS

Cats' ears range from small to large, wide to narrow at the base, set high to low on the head, with pointed to rounded tips. For example, the Scottish Fold has small, forward-folded ears. Medium-sized ears are found on the Burmese, while the Cornish Rex has tall ears set close together.

The Oriental Shorthair has a wedge-shaped head and unusually large, pointed ears.

TAILS

There is no really good functional explanation for a cat's tail, although it may help with balance. Some species have dispensed with their tails almost completely.

The tail markings of most cat species include rings and tips in a contrasting color. These may serve to make signals more obvious when a cat swishes its tail as a threat. Domestic cat tails come in many sizes and shapes. The Japanese Bobtail has a short tail resembling a pompom. The Cornish Rex and Siamese have long, slender tails. The Turkish Angora and the Ragdoll have long, thicker tails. Other breeds, such as the Burmese, Exotic and American Shorthair, have medium-length tails. The Manx is the best-known tailless breed, although many do have some vestiges of a tail.

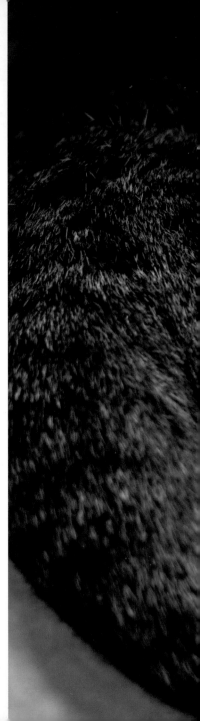

The Sphynx has a long, tapered hairless tail.

This tabby's tail is marked by bands and ends in a black tip.

EYES

White cats with blue eyes are more likely to suffer from deafness than other cats.

Cats have large eyes for their skull size. Domestic cats' eyes are almost as large as human eyes. Those of nocturnal species are especially large to gather light.

Cats rely heavily on sight and have excellent night vision and a wide visual field. The pupils are able to dilate fully to a circle in low-light conditions, but in sunshine they contract to vertical slits to protect the sensitive retina. Cats' eyes are extremely sensitive to light because they have a layer of reflective cells, found in many nocturnal animals and almost all carnivores. This layer reflects the light back through the sensory cells to double the effect of each photon of light. While this makes the eyes more sensitive, the reflected image is not perfect and appears blurred.

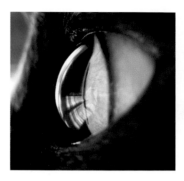

Cats' eyes face forward, giving them good stereoscopic vision.

Abyssinian cats have gold, green or hazel colored eyes.

SMELL

A cat's sense of smell is important for communication, as they scent-mark their territory. However, when cats hunt they rely more on their vision than on smell.

If a cat's sense of smell is affected, such as when its nose is congested by 'flu, the cat may refuse to eat or will be tempted only by pungent foods, such as smoked fish. Their toilet habits and scent-marking can also be upset. In addition to the usual nasal sensors, cats (and other carnivores) have an auxiliary olfactory membrane located in two canals, one behind each incisor, leading from the roof of the mouth. This sensory organ isn't fully understood but seems to be used by male cats to check a female's readiness to breed.

Cats detect chemicals with their sense of smell. The sensitive whiskers detect by touch.

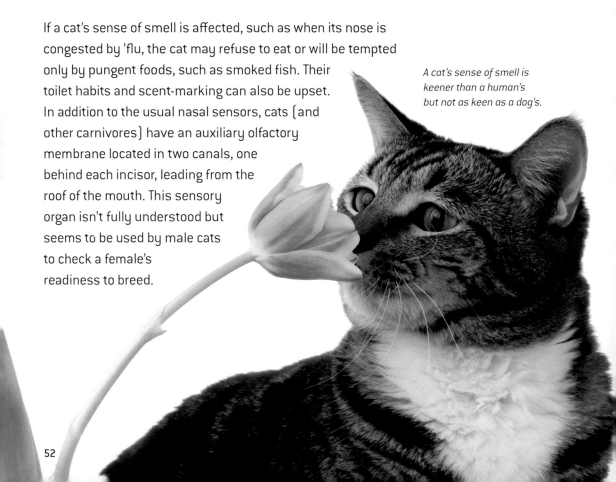

A cat's sense of smell is keener than a human's but not as keen as a dog's.

Cats purr when content, but also when injured and even when giving birth.

BODY LANGUAGE
Hissing • Vocalizing • Purring

Unlike humans, cats can't mask their feelings. As you get to know your cat, you will begin to understand what he says with his body and his various vocalizations.

Meows have subtle differences that owners soon learn to understand.

HISSING

When confronted by a perceived threat, a cat's first reaction is to draw back and hiss. If the threat continues, he either flees or moves into fight mode, growling and fluffing up his coat and tail.

An aggressive cat arches his back, fluffs up his fur and spits.

VOCALIZING

Cats learn that meows and purring often get them food and attention from their owners. Some breeds are more vocal than others—Siamese cats are notorious for emitting piercing wails at night. The short "chirp" usually indicates pleasure.

PURRING

It isn't clear why cats purr, but it seems to keep the air sacs open during shallow breathing. It is thought to express pleasure, and to have a calming effect.

BODY LANGUAGE
Meeting • Submission

Cats have particular ways of approaching each other when they meet and behaving when a confrontation occurs. This often saves them from being hurt in a fight.

When cats meet, they approach each other warily.

MEETING AND GREETING

When two friendly cats meet, they touch noses, gathering information by sniffing each other from face to anus. (Your cat may greet you by sniffing your nose and face.) During the greeting the cats appear wary, their necks stretched out and their bodies slightly crouched.

Cats show affection by rubbing against each other, just as they rub against their owner's leg.

SUBMISSION

When a confrontation between two cats takes place, they hiss and stare each other down. They may fluff themselves up, or one may turn side-on to the other to appear larger. One usually backs down, crouching low and flattening her ears, then moving away or rolling onto her back to avoid a fight.

When a cat does not want to fight, she crouches to show submission, but remains alert.

BODY LANGUAGE
Ears • Eyes • Tail

Cats use body language to communicate with each other and to show how they feel. By learning these signals, humans can understand their cats better.

EARS

Your cat's ears move to catch sounds, but their position also conveys messages. An alert cat pricks his ears. A threatened or angry cat flattens his ears down and sideways. If feeling playful, he pulls them down and to the back.

EYES

When a cat is angry, excited or frightened, his pupils dilate, going from a straight line to round. When alert or anxious, he blinks rapidly. During a confrontation with another cat, or while preparing to attack prey, his stare is unwavering.

TAIL

A cat's tail is a good indicator of mood—an angry cat swishes his tail, a straight and high tail tells you he's relaxed, but a horizontal tail may mean that he is feeling stressed.

Ear, eye and tail movements combine when a cat pounces.

When stalking, a cat stares intently at his target prey.

AGGRESSION

The white cat's claws are retracted, so this is a game between friends, not a serious fight.

While cats tend to avoid fighting, there are some cases where it is the only way to retain their standing in the cat hierarchy. Unfortunately, the loser risks getting bitten or scratched.

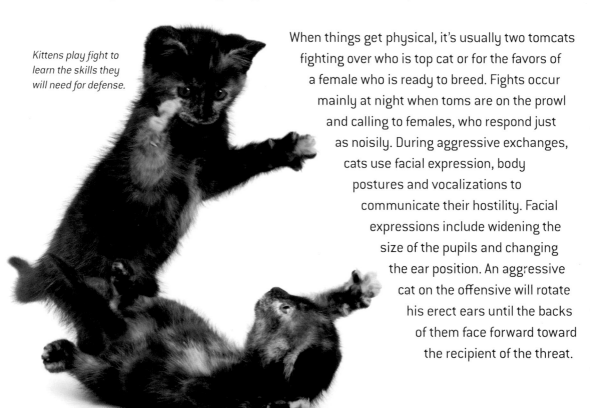

Kittens play fight to learn the skills they will need for defense.

When things get physical, it's usually two tomcats fighting over who is top cat or for the favors of a female who is ready to breed. Fights occur mainly at night when toms are on the prowl and calling to females, who respond just as noisily. During aggressive exchanges, cats use facial expression, body postures and vocalizations to communicate their hostility. Facial expressions include widening the size of the pupils and changing the ear position. An aggressive cat on the offensive will rotate his erect ears until the backs of them face forward toward the recipient of the threat.

HUNTING

Hunting cats crouch low and stalk their prey, pouncing with a sudden rush and biting the victim in the throat. This method is almost universal among cats.

Cats are valued for killing rodents but their owners usually don't want them to kill birds. Some owners attach bells to their cat's collar to warn the birds, but this is often ineffective. It is best not to encourage birds into your garden, as the cat is only doing what comes naturally. Similarly, when a cat plays with her victim, she is merely stunning it so that it can't run away. If it lies still, the cat loses interest. If you are trying to rescue a bird or other inappropriate prey, distract your cat by creating movement nearby in the bushes.

Cats are intrigued by anything that moves, including goldfish.

Cats are patient predators. They will sit silently, motionless, waiting for their prey.

COMMON BEHAVIOR PROBLEMS
Scratching • Biting

Cats need to scratch to mark territory and keep their claws in good condition.

To train your cat not to do certain things, you must first try to understand why he does them. Some behavior problems can be easily dealt with, while others take perseverance.

SCRATCHING

Because scratching is natural marking behavior, the best solution is to provide a scratching post. Encourage your cat to use it by rubbing dried catnip into it to make it smell inviting and placing it where he likes to scratch. Cover scratched furniture until he likes the scratching post better.

It can take time and understanding to cure a cat of a biting habit.

BITING

Some cats that weren't sufficiently socialized with humans as kittens switch from seeming to enjoy being petted to attacking their owner's hand. Perhaps they suddenly feel trapped, so don't try to hold the cat in your arms. Instead, let him come and go freely on your lap until he is confident.

COMMON BEHAVIOR PROBLEMS
Jealousy • Stealing Food

Both jealousy of a newly introduced pet and food stealing
are common problems with cats. Some simple strategies
can help cat owners deal with them successfully .

JEALOUSY

If you obtain a new pet, your cat might see it as an intruder.
Most pets accept others eventually; meanwhile limit their
contact and spend plenty of private time with each one. Cage
the newcomer and feed the animals together from separate
bowls. With food to distract them, they will be less hostile.

STEALING FOOD

The best way to stop stealing is not to leave food unattended.
But there will always be times you forget. When you catch
your cat in the act, make a loud noise by
hitting the table. Your cross voice and body
language will deliver the message.

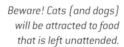

*Given time, most pets will
warm to each other.*

*Beware! Cats (and dogs)
will be attracted to food
that is left unattended.*

SPRAYING

Although spraying is a natural way of sending messages, it can cause problems for owners. You and your cat may have to make some compromises to work things out.

Cats are conscious of their territorial rights and spraying the boundaries is just one way of sending "keep out" messages to interlopers, along with making scratch marks, leaving feces unburied and rubbing secretions from the sebaceous glands on the skin of the side of the head on building corners. While both sexes spray, the urine of males, especially that of tomcats, is more offensive. Owners don't really appreciate the pungent stink of urine on or around doorways or indoors, and some garden plants can be killed.

Scent markings warn other cats to stay away and can prevent fighting.

Marking a territory is a natural behavior for cats in the wild, as this tiger displays.

Cats constantly renew their territorial scent markings.

THE CAT IN YOUR LIFE

BECOMING A CAT OWNER

OWNING A CAT CAN DO wonders for a person's health and happiness. Of course, caring for any pet is a big responsibility and food and veterinarian bills can be expensive, but all the effort you put into caring for your cat will be repaid by years of companionship and love.

If you spend time away from home, it can be good to have more than one pet to keep each other company.

CHOOSING A CAT

Only a few cat owners want to breed and exhibit purebred cats, which can be expensive. Most are looking for that special cat to share their heart and home.

When choosing a kitten, make sure he has clear eyes and a healthy coat.

Before you acquire a cat, ask yourself if you are willing and able to provide for him for some 18 years. Do you have a safe environment in which he can live? Do you have time to groom and care for him? Are your children trained in the responsibilities of pet ownership? Will your other pets accept a newcomer? Can you afford food and veterinary care? If you answered yes to these questions, you're ready to become a cat owner.

Many cats make excellent companions and playmates for families with children.

WHERE TO GET YOUR CAT

A new cat or kitten will soon become a part of your household.

There are many places where you can acquire a cat. Where you go depends on the type of cat you want, and whether you prefer a purebred or mixed breed.

Many people like the idea of giving a homeless cat a place to live. Rescued cats are available from animal shelters, although they don't always know the cat's history. Cats are also advertised in newspapers or on vet's bulletin boards. Pet store cats should be well looked after and the store should offer you health guarantees.

Purebred cats are available from private breeders and catteries or at cat shows. When buying from a breeder, make sure that their house is animal friendly. It's good to see the kitten's parents, as this indicates what your cat will be like when grown.

Many cats end up in animal welfare shelters and need good homes.

When buying a purebred kitten, ask for its pedigree record.

A KITTEN OR OLDER CAT?

There are important considerations to take into account when trying to decide whether an adult cat or a kitten will suit your home and family best.

Kittens adapt easily to new homes. For this reason, it is best to choose a kitten if you have other cats. When bringing a kitten into a house with children, encourage the children to stay away until she approaches. Supervise them until you are confident they are mixing safely together.

Many adult cats need loving homes. They adapt more easily to a new home with no other cats. Cats and children mix well—an older cat will simply move away if playtime becomes rough. An adult isn't as boisterous as a kitten and will make a suitable companion for an older person.

Kittens will adjust to a home with other cats, but they should be supervised.

Adult cats can take some time to adjust to a new home.

PUREBRED OR MIXED BREED?

There are many things that could make you want a particular cat. You may have a friend with an adored pedigree Bombay or you may simply prefer a mixed-breed cat.

Russian Blues are known for their affectionate nature.

The hairless Sphynx must be kept warm and out of the sun.

A purebred cat may appeal to you because of its color, coat or body shape. This is the main charm of a pedigree cat—while all cats are individuals, purebred cats are more likely to live up to a breed's characteristics and quirks. For instance, Siamese just love to play and follow their owners around. Russian Blues are known to be extremely affectionate.

There are far more mixed-breed cats in the world than purebreds and many are more beautiful. These cats tend to be hardier and are easier to care for. They also cost a lot less.

Mixed-breed cats generally have fewer health issues and special requirements than purebreds.

Persians are quiet and loving, but need daily grooming to keep them in good shape.

HOW TO HOLD A CAT

It is important to know how to pick up a cat correctly to ensure that you don't cause him any harm or distress so that he continues to enjoy interacting with you.

You can safely pick up a kitten by the scruff of the neck while supporting him with your hand underneath his body. Never pick up an adult cat this way. To pick up an older kitten or a small cat, support his weight from underneath, holding him securely to your chest with the other hand. If he is a large cat, pick him up by placing one arm under his body from the rear, with your hand coming up between his front legs. Support his weight and hold him firmly. Never pick up a cat by his leg or tail.

Kittens may be safely picked up by the scruff of the neck.

Kittens need to be treated gently at all times to prevent injury.

Always fully support the weight of an adult cat, and hold him firmly if you don't want him to escape.

83

BRINGING YOUR CAT HOME

Both kittens and adult cats need time to adapt to new environments. They will be afraid, so make sure you provide a comfortable introduction to your home.

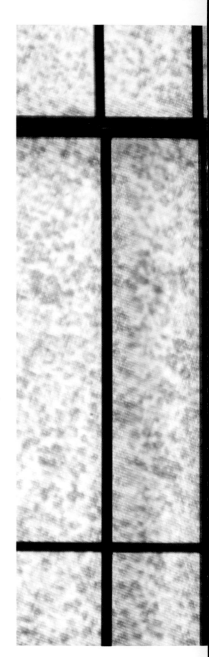

Use a carrier to transport your new cat home because if you carry her in your arms she could claw her way free. If you are driving, a scared cat running loose in the car could be dangerous.

When you arrive home, confine your new cat to a room but don't leave her shut away by herself. Even if you want an

To keep your new cat secure, bring her home in a carrier.

indoor/outdoor cat, you should never put a new cat outdoors until she is ready. Always leave a litter tray in the room, as she won't want to explore her new home for the first few days.

Keep your new cat indoors . When she is used to one room , let her explore the rest of the house.

YOUR NEW KITTEN

Your kitten will need a lot of love and attention. Since he no longer has siblings to play with, you will in effect become his sibling.

Always play gently with a kitten to avoid frightening him.

Your kitten will wrestle your hand, kick and gently nibble you. This is the way in which he burns off excess energy. If his bites become harder, discourage him by saying "No!" firmly or by blowing softly into his face. Until he is used to you, always talk softly and move slowly. A scratching post is essential if your cat is to remain indoors. An outdoor cat will use the trunk of a tree. It is important to provide cats with a warm and dry bed, big enough for the cat to stretch out in when fully grown.

Provide a bed for your kitten, though he may choose his own place.

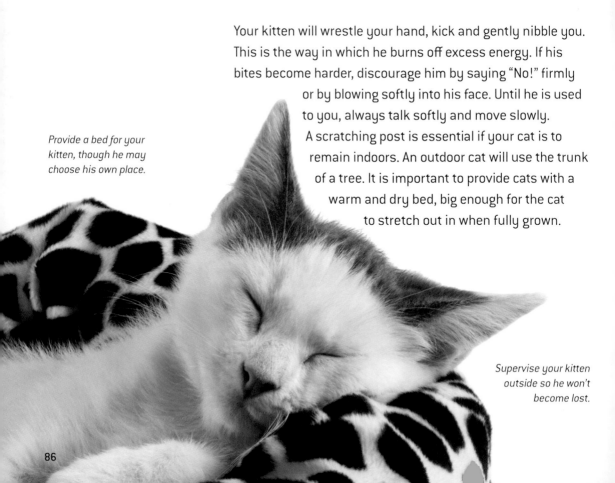

Supervise your kitten outside so he won't become lost.

YOUR NEW ADULT CAT

Cats don't like change and patience is the key to helping your older cat adjust to a new home. To help her, avoid talking loudly and don't make sudden movements.

Your primary concern is to ensure that your cat has a safe refuge from people and other pets. She will probably seek out a hiding place. Provide her with water and food dishes and a litter tray. If she hides under furniture, place a cat bed or small blanket there for her comfort. She will not use a cat bed in the open until she feels secure. There is no telling how long it will take for your cat to feel comfortable. Some cats come around within a few days while others may take months.

If your cat is too frightened to come out from hiding, try sitting nearby and talking quietly to her.

Don't try to pick up a frightened cat against her will.

MEETING OTHER PETS

Don't turn your new kitten loose with your other pets as soon as he arrives home. His most important needs are to feel secure, eat normally and use his litter tray.

Despite their reputation for hostility, cats and dogs can become friends.

It helps to introduce cats and dogs when they are young.

One way to introduce your kitten to other cats and dogs is to put him in a room with a screen door or set up a temporary cage so he can meet them without having any spats. Otherwise, turn him loose in the house after a few days to see how the other animals accept him. It is normal for them to hiss and spit. A kitten will not fight and is used to his mother hissing at him when she has decided he no longer needs to nurse. Unless hopelessly trapped, your kitten will simply walk away.

If properly nurtured, cats can live with other animals.

Stay on guard with your new cat until you are certain your pets are mixing safely.

INDOOR OR OUTDOOR?

If you live close to busy streets, you may wish to keep your cat strictly indoors. If you have a yard, however, you may prefer to have an indoor/outdoor cat.

Play stimulates indoor cats and helps them stay alert and healthy.

There are certain points to consider before making this decision. If your cat is kept strictly indoors, he will become totally dependent and domesticated. He could be a perfect companion but will require a lot of attention as he won't have the neighborhood to explore.

Cat flaps allow cats to enter and leave the house at will.

However, if you allow your cat to be an indoor/outdoor cat, he may never fully develop into a domestic companion. For his own protection, he must retain many of the wild instincts necessary for survival. For instance, even if he is neutered, your cat may sometimes mark his territory by spraying when he enters the house.

Indoor cats need access to natural sunlight and fresh air.

DANGERS OUTSIDE

Even if you have an enclosed yard, your outdoor cat may encounter dangers ranging from being attacked by dogs or other cats to being struck by a car.

Stay with your kitten outdoors, as he is vulnerable to danger.

Your cat can easily wander out of the yard just as other cats can wander in. For this reason, your outdoor cat should be neutered. If your male cat is unaltered, check him frequently for wounds inflicted by other tomcats. If your female cat is unaltered and has kittens, she will need to be provided with a secure retreat. If you have a farm cat, he will have to learn the pitfalls of livestock and moving vehicles on his own. As with all cats, make sure his vaccinations are up to date and he has a dry, comfortable sleeping place.

Fences don't provide a barrier to cats, who can easily climb them and roam.

It is best to neuter your outdoor cat to reduce the number of unwanted stray kittens that are born every year.

SPAYING AND NEUTERING

Unless you are planning to use your cat for breeding purposes, it is important to have him or her desexed. There are too many unwanted kittens needing homes.

Your vet will advise you on the best age to have your cat desexed. Generally, while a female can be spayed when she is only a few months old, you should wait until a male is six months old.

The cost of desexing your cat pales in comparison with the potential cost of treatment for wounds as a result of fighting other tomcats, or replacing your carpet or furniture because of spraying. If you are on a limited income and cannot afford the full price, ask your town authorities and local vets about a low-cost neutering program.

Fighting cats can give each other serious bites and scratches.

While desexing your cat is costly, it is far cheaper than repeatedly treating a cat wounded in fights.

THE RESPONSIBLE CAT OWNER

A contented cat is happy simply to be in her owner's company.

Before you acquire a cat, you have to remember that she may live for more than 18 years. Having one is a major responsibility and requires dedication, time and money.

Cats may behave instinctively and not to their owner's liking.

Cats can be excellent family pets, but children need to be taught to treat them with respect.

Cats give us love and companionship. In return they must be provided with a safe and clean home, food, grooming, medical care, and of course, to be loved in return. There are also a number of practical and legal issues to be considered. Possibly the most important need is to register your cat and fit her with clear and secure identification, such as a collar and tag, in case she gets lost. Another option is having a microchip implanted. This identifies her to any vet or animal shelter with the proper scanning device.

CARING FOR YOUR CAT

CATS MAKE WONDERFUL PETS, but like all pets they need to be well cared for. They need to be fed healthy food, to be given a space of their own, to be groomed and have their health checked. You will need to make some adjustments to your home to allow for their special requirements.

Cats, like all pets, look to their owners to care for them and make their lives safe and happy.

A SAFE HOME

When you take a cat into your life, you must be prepared to provide for her every need. Just as you would with a baby, your house needs to be safe to avoid accidents.

Having the right equipment will make life easier for you and your cat, but don't rush out and empty the local pet store. Start with just the basics and add things as you find you need them to keep your new companion safe and healthy. Cats are very self-sufficient, so don't be daunted. The main thing is to provide her with a safe environment. Think of her as a toddler and take the same precautions you would with a child, such as locking cabinets with dangerous contents and blocking off danger zones that, inevitably, seem to have a fatal attraction.

Verandas and upstairs windows need rails to prevent accidental falls.

Kittens are active and playful. Provide safe toys for them to play with.

If you have an open fire, always have a sturdy fireguard that can't be easily knocked over.

BEDDING

Covered cat beds provide additional warmth and an extra sense of security.

Most cats do a lot of sleeping and prefer the security of a sleeping place above floor level with a solid wall at their back. Your cat may well choose his own place to sleep.

Ring pillows offer warmth on a cold, uncarpeted floor.

You can make a warm, comfortable sleeping place for your cat on a piece of furniture, preferably against a wall. Some cats like sleeping on top of the refrigerator or the washer or dryer. The heat from these appliances will keep him warm. He may decide that the floor or shelf of a dark, quiet closet suits him. Simply leave the door slightly ajar for him to come and go. Wherever he decides to sleep, make it comfortable by providing him with a ring pillow—a round, stuffed pillow, with sides about 4 inches (10 cm) high.

Your cat may choose an upholstered chair to settle down on.

LITTER AND LITTER PANS

For the comfort of yourself and your cat, consideration needs to be given as to the kind of litter pan and litter you provide. The pan will need regular cleaning.

The size of your cat's litter pan depends on how large she is and if she will be sharing it with any other cats. You can choose a plastic pan from several sizes at any pet store. Simply line the pan with a section from the newspaper and then cover with strips torn from another section. After the cat uses the litter pan, it is easy to roll up the entire newspaper and dispose of it. You can also use sand, clay or wood shavings as the actual litter but these materials might end up being trekked through the house.

Put her litter pan in a quiet place so your cat won't be disturbed.

While a scoop allows you to remove solid material easily, don't leave wet litter for days at a time or it will begin to smell.

BOWLS AND SAUCERS

Like people, cats need access to clean food and water. A number of options are available for providing your cat with a good supply of both.

Bowls should be wide at the base so they are not easily tipped over.

Double feeders allow you to keep different foods apart.

Your cat will need bowls for both water and dry food, and a flat saucer for moist or wet food. If you have more than one cat, or if you are feeding outdoor cats, a water feeder and a dispenser for dry food are excellent. These can hold a larger amount of water and food than bowls and have protective covers to keep the contents fresher and free from dirt. A water feeder is also useful if you are away from home for several hours at a time, because your cat won't be able to knock over his water source.

If you have more than one cat, it is good to provide more than one bowl to prevent competition.

SCRATCHING POSTS, COLLARS AND HARNESSES

Depending on whether you have an indoor or outdoor cat, these items can be important pieces of equipment that will make your life easier and keep your cat safe.

Attach a leash to a harness as collars are easy to escape from.

If you have an indoor cat, it is vital that you purchase a scratching post or pad to replace the trunk of a tree. The post should be taller than she is long with her front legs stretched forward.

Outdoor cats should wear a collar with a break-away feature to keep them from being strangled if they become snagged. A leash is needed if you want to train your cat to take walks. It should be of a light material and be suitable for her size and weight. Only a figure-8 cat harness should be used with the leash.

A scratching post may well save your furniture from being destroyed.

If your cat spends time outdoors a collar with identifying tag means she can be returned to you if she becomes lost.

110

Grooming gloves allow you to brush your cat while stroking him.

TOYS AND GROOMING EQUIPMENT

Both play and grooming are opportunities for you and your cat to enjoy time together, so toys and grooming equipment are important investments for your cat.

Simple, safe toys may stop your cat playing with your possessions.

There are many cat toys on the market. Although the best ones have you attached, your cat will need toys for when you're away or too busy to play with her. When purchasing a cat toy, make sure it is free of small attachments that can detach and be accidentally swallowed.

Your cat will need her own combs and brushes. The types you buy will depend on whether she has a short or long coat and fine or thick hair. Cotton swabs for ear-cleaning are a must, as well as scissors or clippers made especially for trimming claws.

Combs are needed for long hair, but care needs to be taken as they can be sharp.

Cats love to play. It keeps them engaged and gives them exercise.

CAT FLAPS

Cats soon learn to use a cat flap. They can be locked shut to keep cats in at night.

If your cat is allowed outside, a cat flap makes an excellent door. They range from models that can be fitted to a screen door, to solid wooden ones.

Some cat flaps can be opened only by an electronic chip on your cat's collar. This stops other animals from entering.

To train your cat to use the flap, prop it completely open. Leave him inside and position yourself outside, directly in front of the flap. Call to him, holding his favorite food. Once he is through, go inside and repeat the process until he willingly goes through. Repeat the process with the flap lowered halfway so he has to push it aside. Once he uses the partly closed flap without hesitation, repeat with the flap down.

Outdoor cats need to get inside to eat or to escape from bad weather.

GROOMING SHORTHAIRED CATS

All cats need grooming. The time required depends on whether she is an indoor or outdoor cat, longhaired or shorthaired, and whether she is a show cat or not.

Accustom your shorthaired cat to combing every three or four days as soon as you acquire her. Using a comb with small, close teeth, start combing at the back of her neck and work down to her tail, following the fall of hair. Be careful around her hindquarters and other sensitive areas. Repeat using a hard rubber brush. To make her coat shine, finish off by running a damp chamois or silk scarf over it. The natural oils found on your hands are great for making her coat lie flat. Daily petting is almost as effective as brushing.

So-called hairless cats need to be sponged daily to remove oils.

Simple brushes and clippers are all that is needed for grooming shorthaired cats.

GROOMING LONGHAIRED CATS

Grooming a longhaired cat must be thorough and is vital to avoid painful matting of the hair. Make grooming an enjoyable time by using affection and play as you work.

Begin grooming by sprinkling cornstarch (for pale cats) or Fuller's earth (for dark cats) through her coat to make it easier for the comb's teeth to slip through. Use a wide-toothed comb on tangles, paying attention to britches, tail, toes and, turning her upside down, her stomach. Even with good daily combing, mats that twist skin painfully may form. Carefully remove this matted hair with blunt-tipped scissors. Seek immediate help from a cat groomer or vet if severe mats form. Use a soft brush for her ruff and finish off by brushing her hair the wrong way so that it stands out.

As long as you are gentle and show affection, most cats soon come to enjoy being groomed.

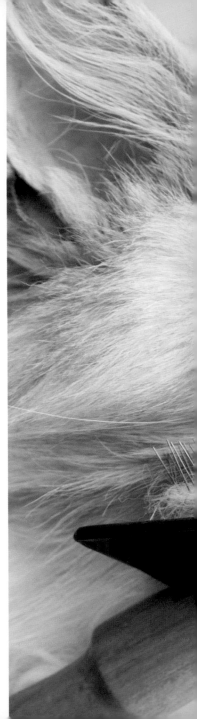

If your cat plays with the brush do not be impatient or you may put her off grooming.

SOILED AREAS

If you have a longhaired cat, you will need to be vigilant about soiled areas, and if you plan to show him, you will need to put in extra effort.

Longhaired cats require special attention to their rear ends.

The fact that your longhaired cat has long hair around his rear end and the back of his legs makes it almost impossible for him to avoid getting clumps of fecal matter on his coat. Tailless shorthaired breeds have the same problem—without a full tail, they cannot sever the feces neatly.

Inspect your cat regularly. If soiled, stand him with his rear end over a basin and wash the stained area with warm water and a mild soap, then rinse him thoroughly. If he has a small amount, pluck it off and then powder him as you comb through the hair.

To get your cat used to having a bath, begin when he is a kitten.

When outdoors, longhaired cats can get grass seeds and twigs caught in their coat.

TRIMMING CLAWS

Start trimming your kitten's claws early and he will learn that it doesn't hurt. Kittens need their claws clipped once a week and fully grown indoor cats every two weeks.

When you squeeze your cat's toe between your forefinger and thumb, the claw will extend and can be trimmed with cat claw clippers. Remove only the very tip and avoid hurting the sensitive pink quick.

While clipping, hold him gently and talk softly. He won't mind you clipping his front claws, but may try to fight when you turn him over to do the back ones. Do not tighten your hold. Pause, talk quietly and try blowing softly into his face while saying "No" in a low, firm voice. Do not let him free until you have trimmed all his claws.

Outdoor cats naturally wear down their claws as they exercise.

Keep a firm but gentle hold of your cat while you trim his claws.

THE IMPORTANCE OF EXERCISE

While cats don't need to be exercised as dogs do, all cats enjoy the companionship of having you play with them. It also strengthens the bond between you.

Kittens chase anything that moves, but need gentle play.

Simple toys that cats can bat and grab provide endless entertainment.

Your new kitten will eat, sleep and, on waking, run about the house like one possessed. This behavior will continue from when she is about six weeks old until she settles as an adult. Don't overtire your kitten, as you can stress her and slow her growth. The best cat toy is one with you at the other end. A bit of string, a belt or anything that dangles is appealing to her. A ribbon trailed enticingly across the floor or in front of her hiding place is sure to elicit a delighted pounce and scamper.

Play helps establish a bond between a cat and his owner.

When cats play, they leap and pounce, exercising their muscles and their instinctive hunting skills.

FEEDING YOUR CAT

Good nutrition is the cornerstone of good health for all pets. With some basic knowledge, it is not difficult to provide the best nutrition for your cat.

Cats must always have access to clean, fresh water.

Cats are carnivores and must eat meat (including poultry and fish) to satisfy their high protein requirement and obtain essential nutrients. They also require many nutrients supplied in good commercial cat foods. Feed your cat in a peaceful, quiet place, away from household traffic and litter boxes. Give each cat a separate dish. It is best to use wide, flat, glass or ceramic dishes with low sides; plastic can cause skin problems. If you have to change your cat's diet, mix a small amount of the new food with the accustomed food, slowly increasing the proportion of the new over three to five days.

Don't feed your cat from your own plate. Many foods that people can eat are dangerous for cats.

Involving children in feeding their cat teaches responsibility.

READING THE LABELS

Feed kittens foods specially formulated for their needs.

Most manufactured cat foods are safe and wholesome. Government food safety bodies regulate the industry and the claims made on labels.

The pet food industry is regulated to make sure cats receive food that keeps them healthy.

The Association of American Feed Control Officials (AAFCO) sets nutritional adequacy standards. So, when choosing food, examine labels for this information:

1 "Complete and balanced" means that all essential nutrients are present in properly balanced proportions.

2 Look for a declaration that the product meets AAFCO standards.

3 The life-stage statement indicates the target group for the food: "All life stages" or "Adult maintenance," for example.

4 Animal protein sources, including poultry or fish, should head the list of dry-food ingredients or, in canned food, immediately follow water. Ingredients appear in the list in descending order by weight.

A good diet is essential for your cat's health. Check out the ingredients in the food you provide.

Pets don't usually need treats, and human food can be harmful. Chocolate, for instance, is highly toxic to cats and dogs.

PREMIUM, CANNED OR DRY?

There are a number of options available for owners to choose when feeding their cat. Should you buy premium food? Is canned or dry food best? And what about treats?

Always refrigerate canned food once the can has been opened.

Dry food must be stored in a sealed bag to stay fresh.

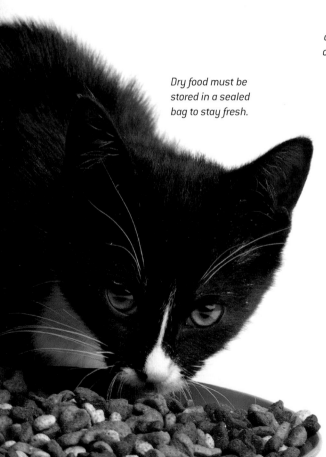

Cat foods sold in grocery stores cost less than premium brands found in pet stores, feed stores or veterinarians. However, high-quality premium foods deliver more energy and are better digested, so can be fed in smaller portions. Feeding your cat dry or canned food is usually a matter of choice. Dry food can be left out. Canned food spoils if not eaten within two hours, so feed at least twice a day. Normally cats on good diets don't need treats, which may cause problems. For example, in quantity, milk will unbalance the diet and may cause diarrhea in adult cats.

SPECIAL FEEDING REQUIREMENTS

Pregnant and nursing mothers as well as kittens have special feeding needs. If these are not met, serious health problems can ensue.

The queen's nutrient demands start to increase early in pregnancy, rising when she is nursing kittens. She needs abundant, high-quality food, AAFCO-certified for reproduction and/or growth. Leave food out or feed her all she will eat several times a day.

When a kitten is three weeks old, start her on canned or dry kitten growth food mixed with cat milk replacer or water. In the following weeks, gradually decrease the liquid in the mixture. After weaning, at seven to nine weeks, feed kittens all they will eat four times a day. At about one year, slowly introduce an adult diet.

Kittens can be free fed by the time they are seven to nine weeks old.

THE KITCHEN

The most important things to train your cat out of are activities that might endanger either him or your belongings. Behavioral training works best for cats.

It is important that your cat does not get into the habit of jumping up on the stovetop in case he gets burned. If you see him do so, give him a squirt with water from a spray bottle. When you are not in the kitchen, cover the stovetop with metal pots and pans. Not only will it be difficult for him to find a place to squat, but the noise they make when he jumps up should send him scampering. You can discourage him from jumping onto tops of the refrigerator and microwave in the same way.

Do not leave food out in the kitchen. Your cat may eat the food or jump to reach it and knock it over.

Cats can be scalded by hot water or food, so keep them away when cooking or washing dishes.

FURNITURE SCRATCHING

Scratching is a natural instinct that all cats possess. Indoor cats are simply scratching furniture to fulfill this need.

Your cat might not be able to distinguish between her scratching post and your chair. If she begins scratching furniture, you can dissuade her using training.

Cover new furniture until your cat learns not to scratch it.

The moment your cat starts to scratch your furniture, give her a squirt from a spray bottle. If she likes water, throw a rolled up newspaper or a bunch of keys on the floor near her. The loud sound and the surprise should stop her scratching. When you are not around, try confining her to a room or pen so she cannot scratch the furniture. If this doesn't appeal, tape orange peel to those areas where she likes to scratch or cover them with clear heavy plastic, or attach a small scratching post to either end of the couch or chair.

WHILE YOU'RE AWAY

Cats don't like change and don't travel well. Whenever possible, make arrangements for your cat to stay at home and avoid sending him anywhere to board.

If your cats live outdoors, oversize self-feeders for dry food and water will suffice for short periods. If you have several indoor cats in good health that do not require extra meals or medication, you can safely leave them alone for a few days. They may be indignant and rearrange your house, so it is best to confine them to one area. Provide self-feeders for food and water, as well as extra litter pans. If you have kittens or older or sick cats needing extra meals and attention, it is best to have someone come in to care for them.

Cats can get lonely while you are away, so arrange for someone to give your cat attention, not just food and water.

Self-feeders keep dry food fresh for some days.

TRAVELING WITH YOUR CAT

Sometimes it is absolutely impossible not to transport your cat, perhaps because you are moving. There are a few dos and don'ts that should make this safer and easier.

If you have to transport your cat by road, always confine her in a suitable carrying cage. When you stop for a break, you can offer her food, water and a litter pan, but don't worry if she refuses all three until you reach the day's destination.

If you are shipping cats by rail or air, first check with the carriers and find out their rules for health certificates and suitable shipping containers. It is not advisable to give cats tranquilizers as they can become aggressive or sick. If heavily tranquilized, vomiting can cause them to drown.

Make sure your cat travels in a secure carrier and that she has access to food and water.

Although a kitten may like to play in a toy car, she probably would not enjoy a real car trip.

141

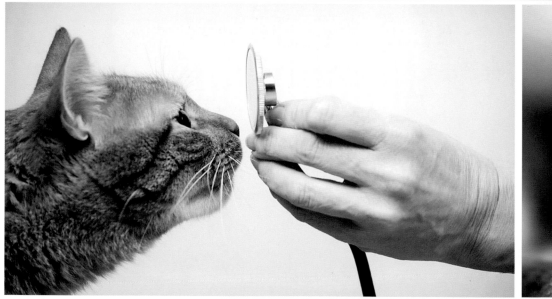

HEALTH CARE

CATS FACE POTENTIAL health problems, such as illness, parasites and accidents but, just as most humans are basically healthy, so too is your cat. Taking your cat to your veterinarian for regular checkups will give you peace of mind and help fix any problems before they become serious.

Food, water, love and a watchful eye will keep your cat healthy and long-living.

THE HEALTHY CAT

Most cats are healthy animals, but a regular checkup by a vet will ensure that your pet is kept in good shape.

When stroking or grooming your cat, look for signs of ill health. If you notice these symptoms, seek advice from a veterinarian. The earlier a problem is detected, the easier it will be to treat.

• If the skin across his shoulders or back stands when gently pulled or falls back into place slowly, he may be dehydrated.

• Lumps on the body may be an abscess or a tumor.

• The rear end should be clean and healthy. Inflammation can indicate diarrhea.

Check your cat's mouth. Redness around the gums may indicate tooth decay or gum disease.

• If your cat is the proper weight, you should be able to feel his ribs easily, but not see them.

• Breath should be fresh and there should be no sign of gum disease.

• Eyes should be clear and clean. The appearance of the third eyelid, or haw, can indicate illness.

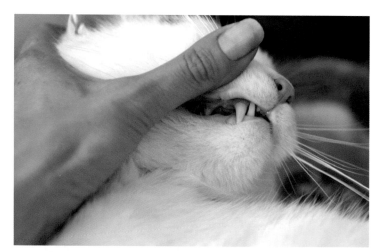

BASIC HOME CARE

The sooner you take your ill cat to the veterinarian, the greater the chance that she won't become seriously ill. You may be able to care for her at home.

At home, the most important thing you can do for a sick cat is keep her warm, quiet, well fed and watered. For an indoor cat, set up a retreat in an unused room. Line a cardboard box with a towel and place it on the floor of a closet with the door ajar. For the outdoor cat, line a tire with an old blanket in a draft-free spot in the garage. Keep her warm using heating pads and hot water bottles (not too hot!). Administer medication prescribed by your veterinarian. If your cat is not drinking, contact your veterinarian promptly.

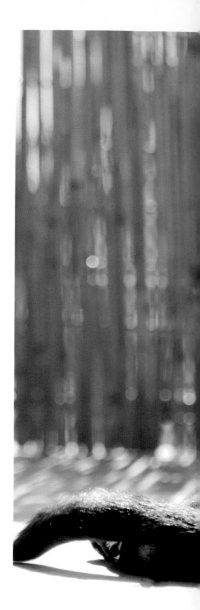

A sick cat needs a warm and quiet space of her own in which she can recover.

Kittens like to be enclosed in their own safe retreat, away from family noise and bustle.

VACCINATIONS

Many serious, even potentially fatal, illnesses can be prevented by vaccination. Some inoculations are compulsory while others are optional.

In the United States and several other countries, all cats must be immunized against feline infectious enteritis, also known as panleukopenia, an often fatal infection of the intestines; feline calicivirus, a respiratory tract infection; and feline rhinotracheitis, also called "cat flu." Initial vaccinations for these should be given at eight and 12 weeks old.

Cats can also be vaccinated against feline leukemia virus, which attacks bone marrow and causes cancer; and feline infectious peritonitis, which causes fluid to fill the chest or abdominal cavity. These extra vaccinations may not be necessary for isolated indoor cats.

A veterinarian vaccinates a cat into the scruff of the neck where the cat cannot reach.

INTERNAL PARASITES

Most internal parasites live in their host's intestines. They can be common and you should contact the veterinarian if you suspect your cat is suffering from them.

All cats, especially kittens, are susceptible to roundworms.

Outdoor cats are particularly vulnerable to internal parasites. Prompt treatment will minimize the damage.

Roundworms are a common feline parasite passed on from the mother or picked up by contact with infected soil or by eating infected rodents. They look like long strings of spaghetti. Symptoms may include vomiting, diarrhea and a distended stomach. The greatest danger is to kittens.

Another common parasite is the tapeworm. All that is visible to the naked eye is the segment, resembling a piece of rice, as it is broken off and expelled through the anus. Cats can be infested through fleas or by eating rodents or rabbits. The best preventive is controlling fleas and limiting hunting.

Pampered indoor cats are less susceptible but may have acquired parasites as kittens, passed on from their mother.

EXTERNAL PARASITES

External parasites live on your cat's skin and feed on both the skin and blood, causing discomfort and sometimes sickness. They are a common problem, but your cat is easily treated.

Cat fleas carry tapeworms and may transmit disease.

Fleas can make cats scratch vigorously and lose patches of hair. They tend to be prevalent around the eyes, ears and anus.

Indoor cats are usually safe from ticks, but outdoor cats should be checked for these parasites.

If your cat has a dark brown waxy substance in his ears or scratches them repeatedly, he may have ear mites. These microscopic parasites feed on skin.

If you detect a tick on your cat, a simple remedy is to cover it with petroleum jelly. The tick usually dies and falls off within a day or two.

Mites cannot usually be seen with the naked eye. They cause mange, the symptoms of which include itchiness, dandruff and bald patches.

All cats scratch and it does not mean they are infested with fleas—but be aware of excessive scratching.

ADMINISTERING A PILL

While a veterinarian can give your cat a pill with confidence, it can be daunting for you to do the same.

Giving your cat a pill is often a difficult chore and cats usually struggle. However, by following the steps outlined below, it will be easier for both of you.

To restrain your cat, have someone else hold him, or, lightly pressing your body against his, place him on a door screen. He will cling on with his claws, leaving your hands free.

Open your cat's mouth, placing one hand on his upper jaw and pushing down his lower jaw with the other. Insert the pill well back in the mouth using the fingers of your lower hand or a pill-popper. Close his mouth and encourage him to swallow the pill by blowing on his nose, stroking his throat, or pinching the skin on his throat and pulling it outward.

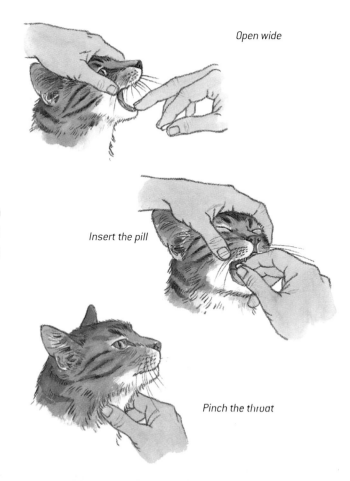

Open wide

Insert the pill

Pinch the throat

ADMINISTERING DROPS

Check your cat's ears for ear mites. A dark, waxy substance or excessive scratching are symptoms of these parasites.

If you are having trouble holding a squirming cat, place her on a table.

Tilt your cat's head while you administer nose drops and until they are well inside the nasal passages. For an ear infection, apply drops into the ear then gently massage its base. To administer eye ointment, pull a lid up or down and lay a strip inside along the length of the lid. Release the eyelid and hold the cat for a few moments to prevent him rubbing. For eye drops, tilt the head back. Gently hold the eyelids apart and squeeze the drops onto the eyeball, keeping the head tilted for 20 seconds to stop the drops rolling out.

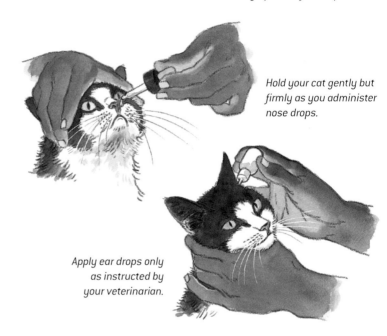

Hold your cat gently but firmly as you administer nose drops.

Apply ear drops only as instructed by your veterinarian.

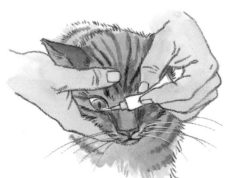

After applying eye drops or ointment, hold your cat loosely.

AFTER SURGERY

Your cat may not like it, but an Elizabethan collar will help him recover more quickly.

After surgery, the best way to stop a cat removing his stitches or bandages is to fit him with a collar that looks as though it comes from the Elizabethan age.

Your veterinarian can provide a collar or you can make one from sturdy, flexible cardboard. Cut out a circle then cut out a smaller one in the center, slightly larger than the size of the cat's neck. It should provide room for movement but not so much that he can remove the collar. Cut away about a quarter of the ring. Punch a double row of matching holes on either side of the gap. Make cuts around the inner circle about 1 inch (2.5 cm) apart. Place the collar around his neck and lace up the opening with string.

You can make an Elizabethan collar or obtain one from your veterinarian.

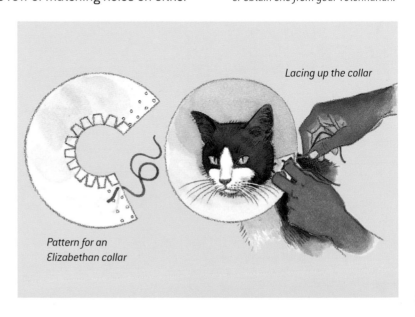

Lacing up the collar

Pattern for an Elizabethan collar

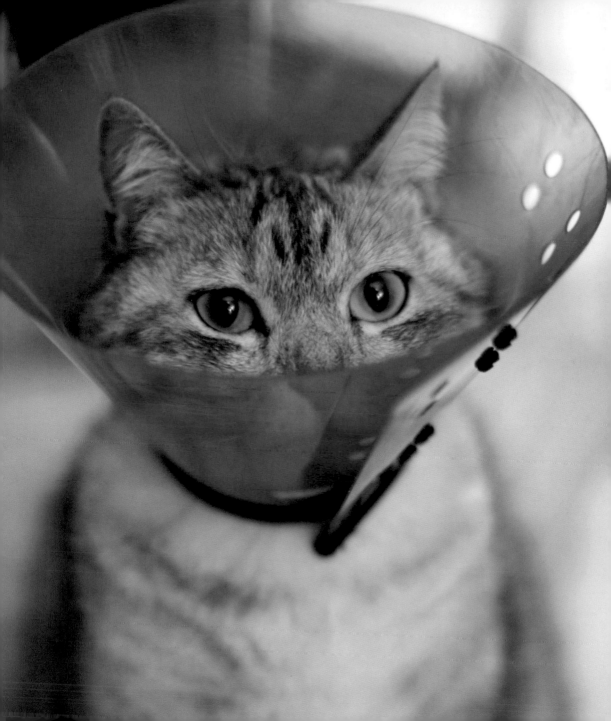

RESPIRATORY AILMENTS

Cats are prone to respiratory problems. Although you will have already protected your cat against the serious "cat flu" with a vaccination, he is still susceptible to other infections.

Early signs of respiratory ailments include watery eyes, sneezing and coughing. You should take your cat to the veterinarian as soon as these signs appear, or nose and chest congestion may develop. Your veterinarian may prescribe antibiotics. The cat may also need to be given eye or nose drops. If he is severely congested, you may be advised to try a bulb-type aspirator.

Although the veterinarian will give the medication that is best for your cat's illness, you will need to provide the tender loving care. He will usually recover far more quickly at home than in the hospital. Follow the general care recommendations.

Speedy professional treatment will get your cat on the road to recovery.

HAIRBALLS

If your cat loses her appetite, has constipation and bowel problems or is vomiting, she could be suffering from hairballs. These form when your cat swallows hair while grooming.

Hairballs are compressed clumps of matted hair.

Hairballs form in the stomach and are then vomited up. They are more common in longhaired cats and when cats are shedding. Daily combing, combined with occasional baths, can aid in controlling hairballs. There are hairball remedies on the market that can help the cat eliminate hairballs by lubricating the intestines, allowing the easy passage of the hairball. Feeding a diet that contains a moderately fermentable fiber source, such as beet pulp, may also help. If your cat becomes very unwell, a hairball may have become impacted in her gastrointestinal tract and may need to be surgically removed by a veterinarian.

While outdoor cats eat grass to get rid of hairballs, indoor cats may need help from their owner.

Longhaired cats are particularly prone to hairballs.

DENTAL CARE

Indoor cats enjoy eating small amounts of cat grass, which may help digestion and oral health.

Cats rarely get cavities but they are susceptible to gum disease. It is important to prevent gum disease because it can lead to bad breath, inflammation and receded gums.

Mouth odor is a good clue to dental problems. It may be caused by teeth that need cleaning or extracting, gum infection or inflammation of the inside of the mouth. Another sign that you cat may have a dental problem is a lack of appetite. His sore gums or an infected tooth may stop him from wanting to eat. Indoor cats may be more prone to mouth problems because they do not have access to outdoor grasses, which act as a cat's dental floss, and seldom chew on small bones, as outdoor cats may. Preventative treatments include massaging your cat's gums and brushing his teeth gently.

You may have to help your cat by brushing his teeth.

Healthy teeth and gums are vital to a cat's wellbeing.

ALLERGIES AND ADVERSE REACTIONS

Anything that causes you to sniffle, cough or itch can have the same effect on your cat. Cats can also have allergic reactions to vaccinations, food or medications.

Cats are most commonly allergic to flea bites. Signs of allergic reactions include itching and hair loss. If your cat shows signs of flea allergy, your veterinarian can prescribe a special diet and/or drug treatment. Be aware, however, that some cats are sensitive to flea preventives. Grooming powders may cause sneezing and watery eyes.

Cats may also react to common cleaning agents, such as bleach and ammonia. These should not be used near your cat unless diluted, and only where there is proper ventilation and the area can be thoroughly dried.

Cats sometimes develop a type of asthma, which your veterinarian can help control.

Skin problems such as dermatitis can result from allergies, so be vigilant in observing your cat's behavior.

Excessive scratching may indicate a flea infestation.

CARING FOR AN ELDERLY CAT

As your cat becomes elderly, you must pay greater attention to his needs. Indoor cats often live up to 18 years. Outdoor cats, however, generally live to around six years.

Although you may not notice because he follows a routine, your elderly cat may start to lose his hearing and eyesight. Call his name before approaching and let him see your hand before you pick him up.

He may develop incontinence, diarrhea and constipation. This can be part of aging, but take him to the veterinarian to verify the cause. If your cat develops bad breath, you should also take him to the veterinarian—it could signify a gum infection or something more serious.

Old cats in reasonable condition should have quality, easy-to-chew food higher in protein and lower in calories.

Your aging cat should not become obese. If he is putting on too much weight, visit your veterinarian to establish an appropriate diet.

FIRST AID KIT

You must take your cat to the veterinarian if an accident occurs. But what if the veterinarian's office is closed? Or the nearest one is hundreds of miles away?

Every household should have a first-aid kit in case of a four-legged emergency. It should include all the items shown here. In addition, you will need the following items when you are away from home with your cat: carrying cage, muzzle, collar and leash, bowl for washing wounds, towel or blanket, tourniquet and sheeting for binding wounds.

alcohol

cotton pads

hairball remedy (paraffin oil)

petroleum jelly

gauze and elastic bandages

hydrogen peroxide

gauze elastic tape

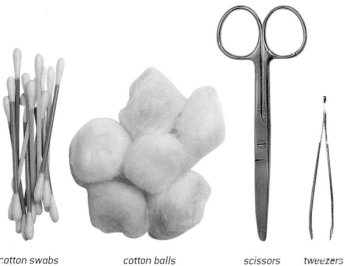

cotton swabs   cotton balls   scissors   tweezers   rectal   eye   plastic

thermometer dropper   syringe

BLEEDING AND BURNS

A makeshift bandage will save the day, but it's important to get professional care as soon as possible.

There are some basic things you can do to treat minor bleeding or burns, but severe cases should always be taken to the veterinarian for further treatment.

For minor bleeding, apply a cold-water compress, put on a gauze pressure bandage and fasten with tape or torn sheeting, never a pin. If your cat is bleeding profusely from a limb or a tail wound, bind a strip of cloth tightly above the wound to make a tourniquet. Take the cat to the veterinarian straightaway.

If your cat is bleeding, apply a pressure bandage to the wound.

For superficial burns, where the affected area turns red and blisters slightly, immediately apply cold water or ice for 20 minutes. If the burn is more serious, the skin turns white and the hairs are easily removed. These burns must be treated by a veterinarian immediately.

To treat minor burns, apply ice or cold water to the area.

TRAUMA AND DROWNING

Cats can easily fall from a height or be struck by a car and can get into difficulties in water. Swift, appropriate action is required to save your cat's life.

If your cat falls or is struck, treat her for shock. Cover her lightly, keep her warm and talk in a soothing manner. Lift her carefully and slowly so as not to worsen any damage. Place her in a small container and take her to the veterinarian. Only a professional can treat such injuries.

Cats are good swimmers but can drown, especially in a swimming pool or even a toilet bowl. After removing your cat from the water, hold her by her hind legs and swing her gently between your legs to expel all water. If she has problems breathing or acts abnormally, contact your veterinarian.

To revive a drowning cat, swing her gently until the water gushes out.

As the saying goes, "Curiosity killed the cat." Be vigilant when your cat is near water.

FEVER AND VOMITING

As with humans, fever in cats can be a sign of serious illness, as can vomiting. Cats with a fever or persistent vomiting must be taken to the veterinarian immediately.

A cat's temperature is normally 101°F (38°). To take your cat's temperature, coat a rectal thermometer with petroleum jelly. Gradually, using a slow, twisting motion, insert it without force about 1 inch (2.5 cm) into his rectum. Hold it in place for a few minutes. If your cat has a fever, take him to the veterinarian immediately. Never give him aspirin.

Cats sometimes vomit due to hairballs, overeating or rushing their food due to competition between cats. Try putting smaller amounts of food in his bowl and make sure he has his own bowl. If vomiting continues, see your veterinarian.

If two or more cats eat from the same bowl, they will compete and eat quickly, which may cause vomiting.

If your cat is listless, not eating or drinking more than usual, he may have a fever.

POISONING

Many household products and some plants can poison cats. If you think your cat has been poisoned, contact your veterinarian immediately.

Most household products that are poisonous to humans will also be poisonous to your cat. Keep such substances out of harm's way. Many common garden and indoor plants are also poisonous. Here is a list of just some of them.

Anemone	Hellebore	Mountain Laurel
Azalea	Hemlock	Oleander
Black Cherry	Holly	Philodendron
Buttercup	Hyacinth	Poinciana
Caladium	Hydrangea	Poinsettia
Castor Bean	Indian Spurge Tree	Poison Ivy
Clematis	Jack-in-the-pulpit	Poison Oak
Crocus	Jerusalem Cherry	Pokeweed
Daphne	Jimson Weed	Rhododendron
Delphinium	Larkspur	Solandra
Dicentra	Liburnum	Star of Bethlehem
Dieffenbachia	Lily-of-the-valley	Sweet Pea
Elephant's Ear	Lupin	Thornapple
English Ivy	Mistletoe	Wisteria
Foxglove	Morning Glory	Yew

Many outdoor cats safely eat grass to help digestion. Some plants, however, can be toxic.

CAT UP A TREE

If your cat becomes stuck in a tree she will usually find her own way down. However, if she is sick or panicked, you will need to step in to get her down.

Try calling and coaxing her into reach with her favorite food or toy. Call your local fire department if you need additional assistance. If these methods fail, it's time to climb the tree. Wear a long-sleeved shirt and thick gloves as she will probably scratch and bite. Take along a small towel to cover and catch her. Stay calm—if she becomes more frightened, she may climb higher.

If all rescue attempts fail, all you can do is leave her favorite food as close to her as possible and keep checking on her to help her down if she needs assistance.

Kittens are curious and adventurous, and sometimes venture beyond their comfort level.

BREEDING AND SHOWING

THE EXCITEMENT OF breeding a cat to meet its standard is addictive. The rewards, however, have nothing to do with money, and everything to do with the cat's beauty and charm. Cat shows offer breeders the chance to compare notes and see fine examples of the various breeds.

The intriguing appeal of the Devon Rex has won it many fans on the show circuit.

THE BREEDING CYCLE

An unsterilized female cat is called a queen—but this owner takes the term rather too literally!

Serious breeders enjoy the challenge of producing particular characteristics in kittens. Their enthusiasm survives late nights and considerable expense.

The outdoor queen may come in season in spring and early fall. The indoor queen, however, may cycle every few weeks due to the artificial light and more constant temperature of her environment.

A queen in season will call loudly to attract a tomcat, crouch and creep about the floor, and may even spray. When selecting a mate, ask to see his pedigree. His ancestors' colors will be listed on the chart. Ensure also that he comes from healthy stock, and is in good health.

To achieve pregnancy, it is best to allow cats to mate over one or two days. Males and females should be separated if they fight between matings.

Unless you are breeding a purebred cat for a specific purpose, it's best not to breed. There are too many unwanted and stray cats.

THE PREGNANT CAT

When your cat becomes pregnant, you'll notice many changes in her, from her temperament to her appetite. This is perfectly natural and not a cause for concern.

Handle your queen gently and avoid taking her anywhere during her pregnancy. If she is listless or shows signs of illness, take her to the veterinarian. At three weeks, turn her on her back. Her nipples should be turning pink and starting to enlarge. Her vulva will also have become swollen.

Prepare a place for your queen to give birth. In a cattery, her cage will be fine. For a house cat, a low drawer pulled halfway out of a dresser and lined with a soft cloth, or a box on the floor of a closet with the door ajar, will suit.

Physical and behavioral changes occur during pregnancy. A pregnant cat may be unusually affectionate.

A cat will generally carry her kittens for around 63 days.

GIVING BIRTH

Your queen will rarely need assistance to give birth. Your veterinarian will be able to give detailed advice on how to care for her during and after the birth.

When your queen is approaching her 59th day of pregnancy, confine her to the cage or room in which she is to deliver her kittens. Signs that the birth is close are plaintive meowing, a tightening of the skin over her abdomen and the movement, or dropping, of the kittens to the rear.

When labor begins, the queen will squat and strain. She should deliver the first kitten within 15 minutes, delivering the rest at intervals of between 5 and 30 minutes. If labor goes on and no kittens appear for more than an hour, or if a kitten or two have been born and labor continues, you should call the veterinarian.

Most cats give birth with little human intervention. Seek professional advice if things go wrong.

The queen delivers her first kitten around 15 minutes after labor begins.

After giving birth, the queen bites off the umbilical cord.

She then cleans and suckles her newborn kittens.

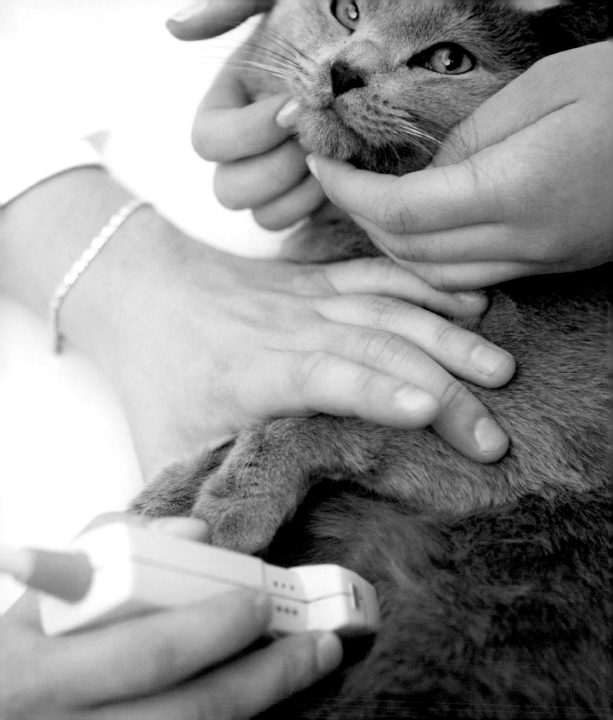

AFTER THE BIRTH

Most queens know instinctively what to do after giving birth, but if it is her first litter she may need your assistance. However, keep intervention to a minimum.

After giving birth, queens immediately open the sacs over the kittens' faces so they can take their first breath. If your queen struggles or doesn't do this straight away, tear open the sacs with your nails. Then place the kitten near her mouth so she can stimulate its breathing with licking. Most queens chew off the umbilical cord, eat the placenta, then wash the kittens. If she doesn't by about 15 minutes, tie string around the umbilical cord about an inch (2.5 cm) from the kitten's stomach. Using sterilized scissors, cut the cord on the side farthest from the kitten's stomach.

The average litter size is four to six kittens, but there could be just one or up to eight.

The queen knows what's best for her newborn kittens.

CARING FOR KITTENS

A healthy queen will ensure that a kitten gets a good start in life.

Kittens open their eyes at between seven and ten days old. At six weeks, they become active. After their first vaccination, most are ready to go to their new homes.

Aside from changing the queen's bedding, feeding her and making sure the kittens' eyes are clean, there is little to do for the first three weeks. Pick the kittens up daily to accustom them to being handled.

If a kitten's eyes don't open by themselves, gently blot them with cotton balls dipped in warm water. A creamy-looking matter is normal and should be cleaned away. Kittens are prone to eye infections.

The queen will naturally discourage the kittens from nursing when she sees fit. They will begin sampling semi-solid food at about three weeks.

Kittens grow quickly. By around three weeks they will be alert and start using a litter pan.

If something goes wrong, you may have to mother the kittens. Kitten bottles can be used to feed them.

SHOWING YOUR CAT

Although plenty of hard work goes into preparing your cat for the show ring, this should also be fun. The thrill of winning a ribbon makes it all worthwhile.

To be shown, all cats must be healthy and free from ticks, lice, ringworm, fleas and all other parasites. They must not have been exposed to a contagious disease within 21 days of the show and must be current on their vaccinations.

Your cat should be bathed and thoroughly groomed before a show. Longhaired cats require weekly bathing and twice-daily brushing between shows to keep their coats in top condition. You will learn some of the grooming tricks over time to ensure that you present your cat as well as possible.

Cats don't have to be purebreds to be beautiful. Many shows include mixed breeds.

To make your cat's neck look thicker, comb out her ruff so that it frames her face.

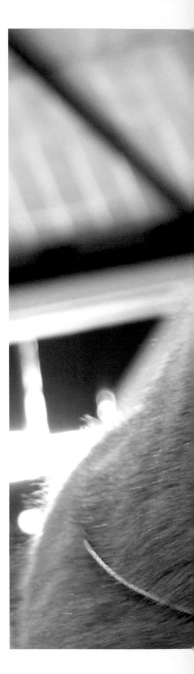

HOW TO USE THIS GUIDE

This guide to breeds is the perfect place to start the search for your ideal cat. With all the relevant information at your fingertips, you're well on the way to finding a cat that's just right for you.

Name of breed
Breeds are presented in alphabetical order for easy cross-referencing.

Introduction
A brief introduction to the breed and its characteristics.

Grooming
Preferred grooming, manner and frequency.

Climate
Preferred climatic conditions.

Hair/coat characteristics
Length and texture in summary.

Temperament
Brief summary of temperament.

Did you know?
An interesting piece of information about the breed.

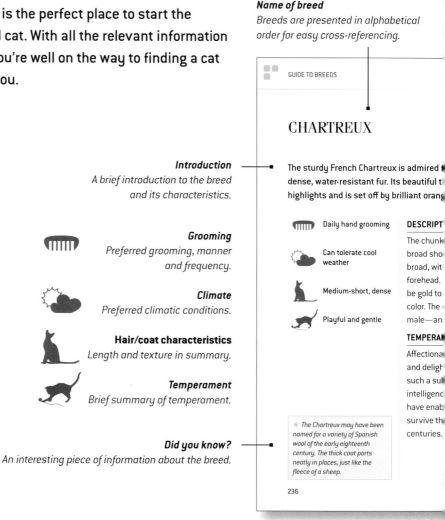

CHARTREUX

The sturdy French Chartreux is admired dense, water-resistant fur. Its beautiful t highlights and is set off by brilliant orang

Daily hand grooming

Can tolerate cool weather

Medium-short, dense

Playful and gentle

DESCRIPT
The chunk
broad sho
broad, wit
forehead.
be gold to
color. The
male—an

TEMPERAM
Affectiona
and deligh
such a sul
intelligenc
have enab
survive th
centuries.

★ *The Chartreux may have been named for a variety of Spanish wool of the early eighteenth century. The thick coat parts neatly in places, just like the fleece of a sheep.*

236

Description
The form of the breed is outlined, including the ideal shape of the body, head, eyes, ears and tail. The length and texture of the hair is also given, along with grooming requirements.

Temperament
This section discusses the breed's general traits and habits to help you decide whether or not this particular cat will fit in with your family and other pets, and with your lifestyle.

Images
A number of varieties of the breed are illustrated in different poses so the reader can easily identify the cat. The animals photographed are not necessarily of professional breeder quality.

CHARTREUX

prowess and its
coat has silver

hartreux is medium length, with
ep chest. The head is rounded and
, full cheeks and a softly contoured
es are moderately wide set and may
nt orange being the most favored
lush—especially thick on the adult
he appearance of both sexes.

he agile Chartreux makes a playful
, but the tiny voice is a surprise in
strength,
ity

The first Chartreux cats were kept by monks at the monastery in Grenoble, France, where the famous Chartreuse liquor was made. The breed was first exhibited in Paris in 1931.

237

ABYSSINIAN

With its sleek coat, the Abyssinian resembles a small wild cat. It is intelligent and active, loyal and affectionate and, although not a lap cat, makes a wonderful companion.

Fawn

 Daily hand grooming

 Moderate climate

 Medium–short, dense

 Active and inquisitive

★ The first Abyssinian taken to Britain was called Zula. Its new owner was the wife of Captain Barrett-Lennard and its picture appeared in a book published in 1874. However, Zula bears little resemblance to today's sleek Abyssinian cats.

DESCRIPTION

The ideal Abyssinian has a slim body of medium size and length. The head is a modified wedge; the ears are large and alert. The almond-shaped eyes are large and expressive, and may be gold, green or hazel with a dark rim. Abyssinians move gracefully and give the impression that they are standing on tiptoe. The lustrous coat is beautiful to feel —soft, silky and fine in texture but also dense and resilient.

TEMPERAMENT

The gentle Abyssinian has a well-balanced temperament and shows a lively interest in its surroundings. It is a great companion cat. Confident, well mannered and responsive, it loves to play and will devise spontaneous little games to hold your attention. It has a small and bell-like voice.

Blue

One of the world's oldest known breeds, the Abyssinian looks like the paintings and sculptures of ancient Egyptian cats. Soldiers returning from the Abyssinian War in 1868 took early specimens to Britain.

Red

AMERICAN BOBTAIL

This relatively new breed has a unique tail that reaches halfway down the hocks and can be curved, kinky or bumpy. It stands upright when the cat is alert.

 Moderate grooming

 Cool to temperate climate

 Medium or long coat

 Friendly and curious

Brown mackerel tabby

DESCRIPTION

The American Bobtail has a brawny, medium-length body. Its broad head has a distinctive brow over deep-set, large eyes. The moderately large, low-set ears have rounded tips. Its double-layered coat has a resilient outer layer and a downy undercoat. The hair can be medium-length or long, with tufts on the ears and feet of longhaired cats. Although the coat does not mat, it needs grooming at least twice a week to remove loose hair.

TEMPERAMENT

Though this cat has a wild appearance, it is good natured and inquisitive. It can learn tricks and games.

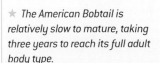 The American Bobtail is relatively slow to mature, taking three years to reach its full adult body type.

In the 1960s, a bobtailed tabby kitten from Arizona was bred to create a bobtailed cat with a coat similar to a Snowshoe. Further work on the breed in the 1980s created the American Bobtail, now recognized by several U.S. associations.

AMERICAN CURL

The backward-tipped ears of the American Curl make it unmistakable. Curious and companionable, these cats adapt to almost any home situation and tolerate other animals remarkably well.

 Quick daily comb

 Tolerates warm or cool climate

 Short, soft, silky

 Affectionate and playful

Brown, classic tabby and white longhair

DESCRIPTION

The American Curl is a medium-sized, elegant and alert animal with a sweet and friendly expression. Its outstanding feature is its remarkable curled ears. At birth, the ears are straight but they begin to curl back during the first ten days of life. The degree of curl is not finally established until the kittens are about four months old. Care should be taken when handling the ears—never force the ear into an unnatural position or you may break the cartilage.

TEMPERAMENT

Curious and friendly, the impish American Curl enjoys human company and remains playful and kitten-like throughout its life. These cats are very affectionate, even-tempered, lively and intelligent, and quickly make friends.

★ *The ears of the kitten curl and uncurl for several months after birth, and it is not until they are four months old that they are set permanently—either curled or not curled.*

American Curls come in all colors and patterns. Choose from a glistening snow-white with azure blue eyes, or a silver tabby with emerald green eyes. Because it is their unique curled ears that set them apart, any color, eye color or coat length is acceptable for showing.

Silver ticked shorthair

AMERICAN SHORTHAIR

A gentle companion, the American Shorthair has had a place on the hearth of American homes since pioneering days. It gets along well with other family members, including dogs.

 Regular combing

 Can tolerate cold weather

 Short, thick, coarse

 Friendly, intelligent and independent

DESCRIPTION

The medium to large American Shorthair is a true working cat. Its body should be strong, athletic and well proportioned. These cats are not fully grown until three or four years of age, with males usually being significantly larger than females. The head is large with a full-cheeked face, slightly longer than it is wide. The bright, clear eyes are large and wide, with the upper lid shaped like half an almond and the lower lid a fully rounded curve. The ears are set fairly well apart and the expression is both trusting and friendly. The legs are sturdy and well muscled, and the paws are full and rounded.

★ An American Shorthair brown tabby was sold for $2,500 at the Second Annual Cat Show in Madison Square Garden, New York, in 1896.

Silver classic tabby kittens

The ancestors of today's American Shorthairs arrived in North America with early European pioneers. They made themselves useful aboard ships by catching the rats that ate food supplies. Once ashore, they established themselves as North America's own shorthaired cat.

Cream mackerel tabby

Although there is a large genetic component from the British Shorthair in the American Shorthair, the American cats are now larger than their British cousins, with less rounded faces, and longer legs and tails.

Shaded silver

Black smoke

AMERICAN SHORTHAIR
CONTINUED

There are more than 100 colors and patterns to choose from in the American Shorthair, ranging from white through various kinds of tabbies to black.

VARIETIES

At one extreme is the white variety, with its glistening fur, and pink nose and paw pads; at the other is the black smoke, which looks solid black until the cat moves, when its white undercoat ripples through. All have a short coat that is thick and coarse. Grooming entails no more than regular combing to remove dead hair and a wipe over with a damp chamois to make the coat shine.

TEMPERAMENT

No matter what the color and pattern combination, the American Shorthair displays the same even temperament and friendliness. Its robust build and protective coat even lend themselves to walks in the rain. The American Shorthair has a gentle, playful nature, which makes it an ideal choice for families.

Blue classic tabby

White

AMERICAN WIREHAIR

Calico van

A coarse, wiry coat distinguishes this quite rare cat. The American Wirehair is an intelligent and affectionate pet, with a vast range of pattern and color possibilities.

 Occasional light brushing

 Can tolerate cool weather

 Medium, crimped, hard

 Friendly to people and other animals

★ *If you stroke the coat of an American Wirehair in one direction, it feels as soft as silk. But stroke it in the opposite direction, and you will think you are touching a mass of steel wool.*

DESCRIPTION

The Wirehair is a medium to large cat with well-developed muscles, very similar to the American Shorthair. Wirehair kittens are born with tightly curled coats. In the mature animal, the hard, frizzy coat feels springy, tight and resilient. The density of the coat leads to ringlet formation rather than clean waves. Grooming is minimal. An occasional brushing with a soft brush to remove dead hair is all that is required.

TEMPERAMENT

Since the American Wirehair is closely related to the American Shorthair, you can expect it to have the same affable nature. The Wirehair is friendly and plays in a gentle manner, getting along famously with children and with other pets, including dogs. It is quiet and reserved with lovable ways.

The first known American Wirehair was one of a litter of six barn cats born in 1966, in Verona, New York. He was named Adam. Every American Wirehair now traces its parentage back to Adam. The breed is largely unknown outside America.

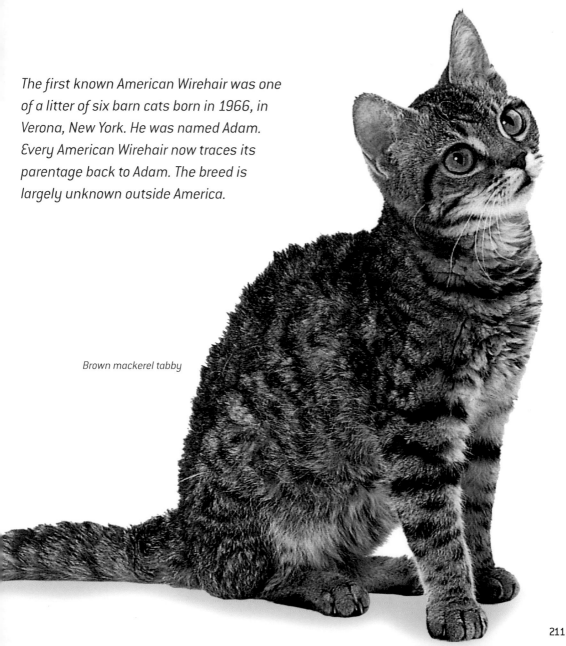

Brown mackerel tabby

211

BALINESE

Chocolate point

With its gently swaying tail, the Balinese is the epitome of natural grace. Intelligence shines in its brilliant sapphire eyes and its inquisitive nature makes it a wonderful pet.

 Regular combing

 Prefers a temperate climate

 Medium–long, fine, silky

 Extroverted and prefers company

DESCRIPTION

The Balinese is exactly like a Siamese except for its coat. It has a long body and is sleek and well muscled. It has fine bones with narrow shoulders and hips, which continue the body's sleek lines. The vivid blue, almond-shaped eyes slant up from the nose. The ears are strikingly large, pointed, wide at the base and continue the lines of the head's wedge.

TEMPERAMENT

The Balinese is intelligent, active and inquisitive, but does not have a loud voice. Some of the longhaired ancestors are perhaps responsible for these cats being somewhat less vocal and having softer voices than the Siamese. They love company and dislike being left on their own; they can be mischievous if they are bored and lonely.

★ The name Balinese was chosen because the graceful way the cats moved reminded their breeder of dancers on the island of Bali, Indonesia.

Blue point

The Balinese looks regal and aristocratic, like a Siamese in a spectacular pale ermine coat. The breed is indeed a mix of Siamese and Angora. Balinese were accepted as a championship breed in the United States in 1963.

Seal lynx point

BENGAL

Seal lynx spotted tabby

With its sinewy body and spotted coat, the Bengal looks like a small leopard—its jungle colors, combined in spotted or marbled patterns, conjure visions of the wild.

 Occasional combing

 Can tolerate a cool climate

 Medium, thick, soft

 Alert and curious

DESCRIPTION

With its large, sleek body, the Bengal looks basically wild. It will wade through water with no hesitation. It is strong boned and very muscular. The large eyes are almond shaped. The ears are short, like those of its wild ancestors. The thick, luxurious medium-length coat is soft and needs only an occasional combing to keep it looking good.

TEMPERAMENT

Offspring of original Leopard Cat crosses and even third- and fourth-generation offspring from the Leopard Cat can revert to the wild and attack without warning. Anyone wanting a pet Bengal should ascertain that it is at least five generations removed from its wild cat ancestors.

★ The Bengal is the only cat with the striking rosette pattern of the wild leopard on its coat.

Today's Bengal was created in the 1970s by a Californian breeder who wanted to reproduce the spotted pattern, colors and facial qualities of the Asian Leopard Cat. Careful consideration should be given before acquiring a Bengal as it could behave threateningly.

Brown marble

BIRMAN

Seal point kitten

A gorgeous cat with sapphire eyes, its long, sumptuous coat and beautiful coloring would be enough to win admirers, but the Birman also has intelligence and a gentle temperament.

 Daily combing and brushing

 Can tolerate cool climate

 Semi-long, silky

 Gentle and quietly active

DESCRIPTION

Ideally, the Birman is long, large and stocky. It has a broad, rounded head with a Roman nose of medium length. The face has a sweet expression, with full cheeks, a somewhat rounded muzzle and a strong chin. The medium-sized ears are set far apart on the head and have rounded tips. The blue eyes are quite round. Its paws are large and round, and all four are white; these are the Birman's distinguishing feature. The tail is bushy and of medium length.

TEMPERAMENT

The gentle Birman has a delightful personality and is active, playful and independent. It makes a good pet for children.

★ *By the end of World War II there were only two Birmans left in Europe. Crossbreeding was necessary to securely establish the breed once more.*

The Birman is known as the sacred cat of Burma. Early in the 20th century, two Birmans were secretly shipped from Burma to France and the Birmans in the Western world all spring from this small foundation.

Lynx point kitten

Lilac point

BOMBAY

Although it was named after the Indian city because of its resemblance to that country's black leopard, the Bombay's similarity ends with the coat. It has a gentle, loving nature.

 Daily hand grooming

 Warm climate

 Very short, close-lying

 Active, friendly and responsive

DESCRIPTION

A medium-sized cat, the Bombay is muscular and surprisingly heavy for its size. Its head is rounded; the face is full with round eyes set apart and a short, well-developed muzzle.
The coat is short and fine. It is easy to groom, needing only regular combing with a fine-toothed comb to remove dead hair, and perhaps a wipe over with a cloth or damp chamois to give it a shine.

TEMPERAMENT

Bombays are smart and agile. They love company, enjoy games and fetch naturally, but may become depressed or naughty if deprived of company. Because they show great affection, they make most satisfying pets.

★ *Although less vocal than many breeds, a contented Bombay rarely stops purring.*

This hybrid cross of the Burmese and black American Shorthair has made the Bombay hardier, healthier and less vocal than many other breeds. Because little hair is shed, these cats are especially suited to a totally indoor situation.

BRITISH SHORTHAIR

A robust and powerful cat with a rich, short, easy-care coat and a calm nature, the British Shorthair is a favorite in Britain, where it originated, and throughout the world. Its genes have contributed to other breeds.

 Weekly combing

 Can tolerate cooler weather

 Short, thick, resilient

 Playful and companionable, but rather reserved

DESCRIPTION

The British Shorthair is a medium to large cat with a compact body and a broad chest. Its round head is set on a short, thick neck. The face is also rounded, as is the forehead, which is slightly flat on top of the head and should not slope. The large, round eyes are level and wide set. The ears are broad at the base, with rounded tips. The short, thick coat is dense. A weekly combing to remove dead hair is all that is needed to keep it looking good, although many owners have a repertoire of tricks to enhance the appearance for show purposes.

> ★ The word "tabby" comes from the name of the old quarter of Baghdad, al Attabiya. Silk fabric patterned in black and white and known as "tabbi" in the West was once made there.

The British Shorthair traces its ancestry to the domestic cats of Rome, which were taken to Britain during the time of the Roman Empire. It is a strong and healthy breed.

Blue

Although the British Shorthair was one of the first breeds to be shown in Britain, it remained comparatively rare in the United States until about 1964, when it was recognized for championship competition there.

Blue spotted tabby

BRITISH SHORTHAIR
CONTINUED

This breed was initially prized for its physical strength and hunting ability but soon became equally valued for its gentle nature, endurance and loyalty.

VARIETIES

The British Shorthair comes in all colors and patterns, except solid chocolate, solid lilac and colorpoint. The tabby pattern is commonly seen in all colors in the classic, mackerel, ticked or spotted tabby form.

TEMPERAMENT

The British Shorthair has a calm, gentle nature and is a loyal pet. Although it can be aloof, it becomes devoted to its owners, and makes a wonderful, undemanding companion that fits in well with family life.

Blue and white bicolor

BURMESE

Sable

Although Burmese have been recorded in their country of origin for more than 500 years, the modern breed dates from the 20th century.

 Weekly combing

 Needs warm climate

 Short, fine, close-lying

 Affectionate, amusing and companionable

DESCRIPTION

The U.S. Burmese is a rounder and more stocky animal than its counterparts in other countries. It has a compact, medium-sized body. The head is a rounded, medium-sized wedge, with a full face. The large, shining, expressive eyes are rounded, set far apart and are a deep gold color. The medium-sized ears are set well apart and have rounded tips. The legs are medium length and are well proportioned with small, round paws in the U.S. (oval paws in Britain) and paw pads in keeping with the coat color. The tapered, medium-length tail should be straight with no kinks.

★ The Burmese is well known for its friendly, affectionate and trusting personality. Because of this characteristic, it should always be kept safely indoors.

A sleek and elegant shorthair, the Burmese is agile and graceful with a delightful personality, good looks and great charm. Easy to look after and playful and tolerant of children, this is, many say, the perfect cat.

Blue

The gleaming coat is short, fine and satiny, and lies close to the body. Grooming entails only a weekly combing to remove dead hair and a wipe over with a damp chamois to enhance the natural shine.

Platinum

BURMESE
CONTINUED

The original Burmese was a sable brown color but breeders began to produce other colors, notably champagne, in the early 1960s.

VARIETIES

In the United States, Burmese come in only four colors— sable, champagne, blue and platinum. In other countries, they also come in brown, blue, chocolate, lilac, red, cream, brown tortie, blue tortie, chocolate tortie and lilac tortie. Sable—also known as brown—is the original and perhaps the most striking color; the lighter champagne (also known as chocolate) is a rich, warm, honey beige color. Blue Burmese have a rich, blue-gray color, while platinum, or lilac, cats have a pale, silvery gray fur.

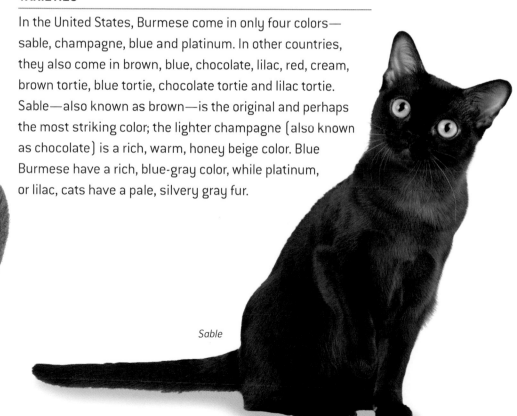

Sable

Champagne

If yours is a household where humans are absent throughout the day, perhaps you should consider keeping two Burmese for company. Females assume an active role in running the house, while males are more laid back and prefer to supervise from someone's lap.

BURMESE
CONTINUED

The foundation animals for this breed were a brown cat from Rangoon in Burma, called Wong Mau, taken to the United States in 1930, where she was bred with a seal point Siamese.

TEMPERAMENT

Burmese are extremely friendly to both strangers and family, and are comfortable with dogs. They communicate in sweet, soft voices, rather like those of the Siamese. They crave attention and affection and will do anything to get it. They remain playful well into adulthood—they have been called the clowns of the cat world—and dislike being left alone for long periods. They are suitable as indoor cats as long as they are given plenty of attention, as they are not as independent as many other breeds. They can form strong and lasting bonds with their owners.

CALIFORNIA SPANGLED

This rare cat has a wild look about it, with its spots and high, wide cheeks, but it has a friendly, curious nature and loves spending time with people.

 Weekly grooming

 Temperate or warm climates

 Short

 Sociable, active, devoted

DESCRIPTION

The California Spangled is long and lean but is quite heavy and well muscled. The short coat comes in various colors, all with dark spots or rosettes on the back and sides. Some are born white and some black, and the spots develop as the cat matures.

TEMPERAMENT

These cats are known to be friendly and devoted to their owners. They are active and are keen hunters that like being in high places. They enjoy playing with toys, especially if their owner is involved in the game. They get on well with school-age children and other cats.

 In 1986, the California Spangled was introduced to the world in a department store catalog, to raise awareness of endangered cat species in Central and South America.

Bred in the 1970s by Californian Paul Casey, the California Spangled was intended to look like a spotted wildcat as he wanted to highlight the plight of wild cats that were being poached for their fur. It was bred from several non-pedigree Asian and Egyptian cats, as well as some pedigree breeds.

CHANTILLY

Originally known as the Tiffany, to avoid confusion with the British Tiffanie, this rare breed has been dubbed the Chantilly/Tiffany in Canada, where it was revived in the late 1980s.

 Weekly brushing

 Cool to temperate climate

 Medium-long

 Calm, quiet, affectionate

DESCRIPTION

Chantilly cats come in chocolate, black, blue, lilac and fawn, sometimes with tabby markings. The semi-long coat has a ruff and longer hair on the backs of the hind legs. It does not shed a lot and resists matting, needing brushing once a week. Wax builds up on the ear tufts, which must be checked weekly. The eyes are golden.

TEMPERAMENT

While becoming extremely attached to its owners, the Chantilly is often aloof toward strangers. It is happy to play with a toy or spend time sitting on a lap. Being so calm, it travels well.

 These cats communicate contentment with a chirp, rather like that of a pigeon cooing.

The origins of this breed are not clear. In the late 1960s, two chocolate-brown, longhaired cats with golden eyes were bought in a pet shop in New York. The buyer, a Burmese breeder from Florida, used them to develop the new breed.

CHARTREUX

The sturdy French Chartreux is admired for its hunting prowess and its dense, water-resistant fur. Its beautiful thick blue-gray coat has silver highlights and is set off by brilliant orange eyes.

 Daily hand grooming

 Can tolerate cool weather

 Medium-short, dense

 Playful and gentle

DESCRIPTION

The chunky body of the Chartreux is medium length, with broad shoulders and a deep chest. The head is rounded and broad, with powerful jaws, full cheeks and a softly contoured forehead. The rounded eyes are moderately wide set and may be gold to copper, a brilliant orange being the most favored color. The coat is soft and lush—especially thick on the adult male—and adds bulk to the appearance of both sexes.

TEMPERAMENT

Affectionate and gentle, the agile Chartreux makes a playful and delightful companion, but the tiny voice is a surprise in such a substantial cat. Its strength, intelligence and adaptability have enabled it to survive through centuries.

> ★ The Chartreux may have been named for a variety of Spanish wool of the early eighteenth century. The thick coat parts neatly in places, just like the fleece of a sheep.

Kittens

The first Chartreux cats were kept by monks at the monastery in Grenoble, France, where the famous Chartreuse liquor was made. The breed was first exhibited in Paris in 1931.

CORNISH REX

Playful and affectionate, the Cornish Rex is distinguished by its unusual wavy coat like that of the Rex rabbit, from which it derives its name. A born acrobat, lively and intelligent, it makes a fascinating pet.

 Daily hand grooming

 Needs a warm climate

 Short, dense, soft

 Affectionate, playful and friendly

DESCRIPTION

Lean and lithe bodied, the Cornish Rex has an arched back and a tucked-up stomach, something along the lines of a whippet. Its head is oval and comparatively small and its large ears are set high on the head. The medium-sized oval eyes are very wide set. The coat is most unusual. It is short, extremely soft, silky and completely free of guard hairs.

TEMPERAMENT

Although it looks wary and sophisticated, the Cornish Rex is extremely affectionate and people oriented. It is an active cat that remains kitten-like well into maturity and it can be very inventive in its play. It likes to fetch and catch, even using its paws to toss small objects.

Blue mackerel tabby

★ *Contrary to common belief, the Cornish Rex does shed hair, triggering allergies in susceptible people just as other cat hair does.*

Black smoke

These unusual cats originated in Cornwall, England—the first Cornish Rex appeared in a litter in 1950. The breed was first recognized for showing in the United States in 1979 and is now accepted for competition worldwide.

Calico

CYMRIC

Also known as the Longhaired Manx, the name of this cat derives from the Gaelic name for Wales, "Cymru," due the idea that there were breeds of tailless cats in Wales.

White

 Daily combing

 Medium-long

 Cool to temperate climate

 Friendly, calm

DESCRIPTION

Having been bred from Manx cats, the Cymric is identical to them except for its medium-length, double coat. This coat comes in a wide variety of colors and patterns and needs daily grooming with a wide-toothed comb. Like the Manx, some of these cats have problems defecating.

TEMPERAMENT

Suitable as a family cat, Cymrics are calm and affectionate. They like spending some time outdoors and are keen mousers. Because they like both high places and shiny objects, some owners recommend keeping jewelry out of sight. Like a dog, some Cymric cats will chase toys and even bury them.

★ *The gene that gives the Cymric its unique tail can also be lethal. Kittens who inherit two copies of the tailless gene die before birth.*

Manx cats have always given birth to some kittens with long hair. In the 1960s breeders in Canada and the U.S. began to selectively breed them. They were recognized as a separate breed there in the 1980s, but are not recognized elsewhere.

Red and White

DEVON REX

The intriguing appearance and charming personality of the Devon Rex appeals to lovers of the unusual and exotic all around the world. Although a comparatively recent arrival on the cat scene, it has already won many staunch supporters.

 Daily hand grooming

 Needs warm climate

 Short, soft, wavy

 Lovable and friendly

DESCRIPTION

The body is small to medium sized; for such a small animal it is surprisingly heavy. The strikingly large ears are wide at the base and set low on the sides of the head. The oval eyes are large and wide, sloping toward the outer edge of the ears. The legs are long and slim and the cat stands high on its feet, almost as if on tiptoe. The coat has a rippling wave effect rather than the tightly waved look of the Cornish Rex.

TEMPERAMENT

Although Devons love to play, they are also content to sit cosily in your lap. They are very affectionate. Devons mature more rapidly than some other breeds and the kittens are strong and mobile at birth.

★ There is a danger of lameness with the Devon Rex and its breeding lines are being monitored closely around the world to eliminate this potential health hazard.

Tortoiseshell

Like the Cornish Rex, the Devon Rex originated from a single kitten, in the 1960s. It has a curly coat and pixie-like appearance. The breed was accepted for championship showing in 1982 and is now being bred worldwide.

Chocolate silver tabby

Blue

EGYPTIAN MAU

Elegance and grace are the hallmarks of the Egyptian Mau. Its beautifully marked coat and well-balanced temperament recommend it as a pet and, as the only natural breed of spotted cat, it also has rarity value.

 Daily hand grooming

 Needs warm climate

 Medium, fine, silky

 Devoted and affectionate

DESCRIPTION

The graceful, muscular body of the Egyptian Mau is medium in length and is very strong. The head is a slightly rounded wedge. The rounded, almond-shaped eyes are large and alert, slanting slightly toward the ears. In adults, they are vivid green but the color develops as the cat matures.

TEMPERAMENT

Very devoted, the Egyptian Mau is not an easy cat to transfer to a new owner. It is intelligent and is thought to have a good memory. Active and playful, it indicates happiness by "talking" in a soft, melodious voice. The tail is expressive and is wiggled at great speed to show delight.

★ *The Egyptian Mau particularly seems to enjoy being walked on a leash. A harness will give you more control.*

Bronze

Thought to have originated naturally in Cairo, the Egyptian Mau (mau means cat) may be a descendant of the venerated cat of ancient Egypt. Three cats were taken to America in 1956 and the breed was recognized for showing in 1977.

Silver

243

EUROPEAN SHORTHAIR

This hardy cat was recognized as a separate breed in Europe only in the early 1980s. Elsewhere, it is not recognized and the British and American Shorthairs remain more popular.

 Weekly brushing

 Cool to temperate climate

 Short, sleek

 Varied temperaments

DESCRIPTION

This cat is highly variable, though is generally not as solid as the British Shorthair and is strong, medium to large in size, with a large, slightly rounded head. European Shorthairs come in a variety of colors and patterns, with eyes that also vary in color. Water stays on the coarse outer coat and is easily shaken off, helping the cat stay dry in rain.

TEMPERAMENT

Though generally friendly, because of their wide ancestry, the European Shorthair does not have a predictable temperament—some are calm while others are active or timid. Perhaps for this reason, they are best suited to homes with older children.

> ★ Many people incorrectly refer to any stray cat as a European Shorthair.

The origins of this cat are ancient and obscure. It is believed to have come from Egypt, and spread via the Roman conquest throughout Europe. In the second half of the 20th century, breeders in Sweden began to deliberately breed their cats to look more like the original Roman cats.

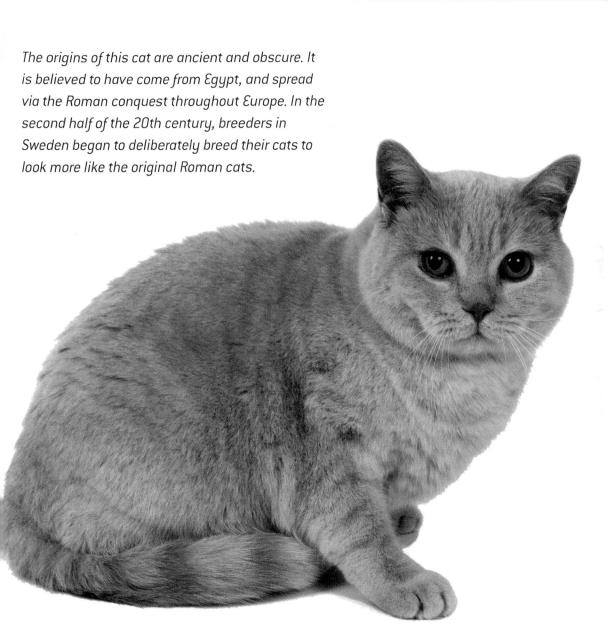

EXOTIC LONGHAIR

While actually being a cross between a Persian and an Exotic Shorthair, this cat looks identical to Persian cats. The breed was registered to distinguish them from Persians.

 Daily brushing, occasional bath

 Cool to temperate climates

 Long, thick

 Playful, active, affectionate

DESCRIPTION

Exotic Longhairs come in the same colors as Persians, and are large with heavy heads. Their long, thick coats require brushing for about five minutes a day. When bathed, they must be blow-dried to prevent the cat becoming ill and the hair becoming badly matted.

TEMPERAMENT

These cats are said to be more playful and active than Persians, but are still gentle. They are happy to live with children and other pets. Because they are known to hide small items such as makeup and jewelry, and to chew things, you may need to "cat-proof" your home.

⭐ *If you want a more outgoing kind of Persian, this cat is for you.*

Occasionally, Exotic Shorthairs give birth to longhaired kittens. Although these kittens look identical to Persians, they could give birth to shorthaired kittens. For this reason, in 1967 this new breed was recognized to keep the Persian line true.

EXOTIC SHORTHAIR

Blessed with a gorgeous coat that is much easier to look after than the Persian's, the Exotic Shorthair appeals to many people. Its temperament shows the best qualities of its varied ancestors.

 Regular combing

 Can tolerate cool climate

 Medium, thick, plush

 A loyal companion, quiet and playful

Black smoke

DESCRIPTION

The Exotic is a heavily boned cat with a stocky body, low on the legs, broad and deep through the chest and massive across the shoulders and rump. Its brilliant eyes are large, round and full, set far apart. The ears are small with round tips, set far apart and low on the head. Legs are short, thick and strong and the forelegs are straight. The paws are large, round and firm, with pads to harmonize with the coat color. The tail is short, bushy and in proportion to the body. Its coat is dense, plush, soft and full of life, with a thick undercoat.

★ *Even experienced cat breeders cannot tell which kittens in a litter of Exotics will be longhairs and which will be shorthairs.*

Before the Exotic was recognized for championship showing in 1967, many breeders of American Shorthairs broke the rules by breeding them to Persians to improve their coats. In 1967 the Exotic was established as a new breed to legitimize this combination.

Red tabby

Although the Exotic Shorthair is very easy to groom, this needs to be done regularly, especially when the cat is shedding its winter coat, in order to avoid hairballs. Comb with a medium-toothed comb to remove dead hair and brush gently with a rubber brush.

Blue cream kitten

White

EXOTIC SHORTHAIR
CONTINUED

Blue kitten

With its appealing flattened face, small voice and easy-care short fur, the Exotic Shorthair is also healthy and long-lived —qualities that make it a perfect family pet.

VARIETIES

The Exotic Shorthair comes in all colors and patterns. Among them are blue, blue-cream, smoke, black smoke, chocolate, pure white and various tabbies and torties. All have the distinctive "teddy bear" face and round eyes of the breed.

TEMPERAMENT

The Exotic has a lively, friendly, lovable nature and seldom makes a sound. It is a sweet and loyal companion, inquisitive and curious, easy to live with and very affectionate.

HAVANA BROWN

The Havana Brown is a gentle creature, rather shy but very loving. Breeders worked hard to achieve this all-brown cat, the challenge being met in different ways in Britain and the U.S.

 Twice weekly

 Warm climate

 Short to medium, smooth

 Quiet and affectionate

★ The Havana Brown possibly got its name because its coat is like the color of the Havana cigar.

DESCRIPTION

These cats differ markedly in body type in the United States, Britain and other countries. In the U.S., the Havana has a moderate-sized, well-muscled body, striking a balance between the cobbiness of the Exotic Shorthair and the svelte length of the Siamese. The head is angular and longer than it is wide. The head of the English Havana is more like that of a Siamese. The short to medium-length coat is smooth, lustrous and needs only to be combed about twice a week with a fine-toothed comb.

TEMPERAMENT

From their mixed ancestry, these cats have a grab-bag of traits to charm their owners. They are curious and characteristically use their paws to investigate, touching and feeling anything that intrigues them. They crave human companionship.

Although breeders had been trying since the 1890s to develop an all-brown cat, it was not until the 1950s that crosses between a seal point Siamese and a black shorthaired cat with Siamese forebears produced the desired result.

JAPANESE BOBTAIL

Familiar to travelers as the cat with the raised paw in china figurines sold in Japan as good luck symbols, the Japanese Bobtail is distinguished by its unusual short tail.

Mi-ke longhair

 Daily combing or brushing

 Warm climate

 Soft, silky

 Intelligent, active and talkative

DESCRIPTION

The medium-sized body is long, lean and elegant. The head appears long and finely chiseled, with gentle curving lines, high cheekbones and a noticeable whisker break. The nose is long with a gentle dip and the large oval eyes are wide set and alert. Legs are long and slender, with the deeply bent hind legs longer than the front; the hind legs are naturally bent when the cat is standing relaxed.

TEMPERAMENT

The Japanese Bobtail is active, intelligent and talkative; its voice is soft and it usually responds when spoken to. It is adaptable, friendly and especially good with children. It loves human company, and has a lively and vivacious charm.

★ *China cats depicting this breed are often placed in shop windows in Japan. They have one paw raised in greeting and are called Maneki-neko, or "welcoming cats." They have long been seen as symbols of good luck.*

Although this breed has existed in Japan for many centuries, it was unknown in other countries until the 1960s. Three cats were taken to the United States in 1968 and the breed was granted championship status in 1976.

Black and white

KORAT

With its silver-blue fur and luminous green eyes, who would argue at the Korat being called lucky? Certainly nobody in Thailand, where the breed has long been esteemed.

 Daily hand grooming

 Warm climate

 Short, fine, glossy

 Affectionate and playful

DESCRIPTION

The muscular body of the Korat is neither compact nor svelte, with males being heavier than females. The chest is broad and the back curved. The head is heart-shaped and very broad across the eyes, unlike any other breed. The prominent eyes are large and luminous green with extraordinary depth and brilliance. The short, single coat is glossy and fine.

TEMPERAMENT

These gentle cats love to romp, but dislike loud, sudden noises. They are calm and sweet-natured and enjoy human company, particularly children, and love to be stroked and petted. Their senses of sight, smell and hearing are unusually acute and they are excellent hunters.

★ *In Thailand, a pair of blue Korats is often presented to a bride as a symbol of good fortune and to bring happiness and longevity to the marriage.*

Although found in all parts of Thailand, the Korat takes its name from one particular province. The first pair was taken to the United States in 1959; at the time the blue coat was spotted with white and the tail was kinked. The breed was accepted for showing in the U.S. in 1966 and in Britain in 1975.

LAPERM

This attractive, easy-care cat came about due to a chance mutation that produced tightly curled hair. There are both short and longhaired varieties. The breed has only recently been recognized.

 Occasional bath

 Cool to temperate climate

 Long, thick, curly

 Outgoing, friendly

DESCRIPTION

Medium-sized but heavy, the LaPerm has a high back. The ears are slightly flared and end in curly tufts. The coat is generally dense, plush and springy. The longhaired version has a ruff, thick undercoat and tail with a curly plume. The cat molts heavily, sometimes even becoming temporarily bald and growing back curlier. The hair does not mat so the only grooming required is an occasional bath.

TEMPERAMENT

Gentle, good-natured and trusting, the LaPerm thrives on human companionship, and will follow its owner around. It is happy on a farm or in an apartment and is a keen mouser.

★ *The coat changes several times before settling into the tight curls that give this breed its name.*

In 1986, an Oregon farmer, Linda Koehl, found an abandoned bald kitten with a strange tabby pattern on her skin. After eight weeks, a curly, soft coat began to grow. This cat, Curly, gave birth to bald kittens that also became curly-haired.

MAINE COON

Large and powerfully built, the Maine Coon is active and good-natured.
Whether it becomes a working farm cat, a household companion or a
show champion, it will always make its presence felt.

Combing and
brushing three times
a week

Can tolerate cold
climate

Long, heavy, shaggy

Loving nature and
talkative

★ *The Maine Coon loves to find
small, concealed places to sleep.
This may be because they once
earned their keep as ship cats.*

DESCRIPTION

One of the largest of all domestic cats, the Maine Coon has a
muscular and broad-chested body that is much longer than
the other longhaired breeds. Male Maine Coons are much
larger and heavier than females. The wide-set eyes are large
and expressive. The long tail is wide at the base with long,
flowing hair and comes to a blunt end.

TEMPERAMENT

The gentle Maine Coon is known for its loving nature, calm
disposition and intelligence, and especially for the soft little
chirping noises it makes. It is
a delightful companion,
loving and loyal and
patient with children.
It is an excellent
hunter and doesn't
hesitate to venture
into water.

Red tabby and cream tabby kittens

The lustrous, dense coat of the Maine Coon is shaggy and, with its slight but definite undercoat, heavy enough to protect the animal from a harsh climate. The coat should be brushed lightly every few days to remove dead hair and stop mats from forming.

Blue classic tabby

261

MANX

The long-lived Manx is famous for having no tail, although many do have vestiges, and for being the symbol of the Isle of Man. It is a charming pet.

Brown patched mackerel tabby kitten

 Daily combing, especially longhairs

 Can tolerate cool climate

 Thick, soft, plush

 Intelligent and courageous

DESCRIPTION

The Manx has the shortest body of any cat breed. The head is round but slightly longer than it is wide, with prominent cheeks and a jowly appearance. Show specimens have no tail, but these are hard to come by. In fact, the last vertebra of the spine is missing, which results in a dip or hollow at the base of the spine where that bone would normally be.

TEMPERAMENT

The Manx is a playful cat and loves to perch on the highest possible point, even indoors. It will retrieve and bury toys as a dog does. It is generally good-natured and friendly.

★ *Two completely tailless Manx cats must never be bred because the kittens are likely to have spinal deformities and die. One parent must have at least some vestiges of a tail.*

Take care when handling a Manx with no tail—never pat the rump roughly as most Manx are sensitive in this area. In spite of their spinal abnormality, however, the Manx is a speedy and powerful runner.

Red classic tabby

MUNCHKIN

For those who must have the very latest, the Munchkin is up-to-the-minute. Admirers of this short-legged charmer, as yet not widely recognized, are confident it has a big future.

 Daily grooming

 Cool or warm climate depending on coat length

 Variable length and type

 Varies with ancestry

DESCRIPTION

The Munchkin comes in every body type, color and coat length. The only thing these cats have in common is their extremely short legs. Since the gene pool is unlimited, there are no clear guidelines as to what type the Munchkin will ultimately resemble. Some Munchkin breeders are mating to Persians, others to Siamese and still others to Abyssinians. In common with short-legged dogs, the front legs are bowed.

TEMPERAMENT

Since the Munchkin has so many different ancestors, its temperament will depend largely upon which cats are on its pedigree. As with any cat, the conditions under which it is raised and the amount of attention given during kittenhood are also factors in the temperament.

Black longhair

★ *The short legs of the Munchkin make it impossible for them to jump to escape predators.*

The Munchkin is a controversial cat. It is the result of a genetic mutation and some believe that breeding should be discontinued; others compare them to short-legged dog breeds such as the Dachshund or Corgi. Munchkins were accorded championship status in the U.S. in 2003.

Tortie and white

NEBELUNG

In German, this cat's name means "mist creature." This describes perfectly the effect of the silver-tipped hairs of the outer coat against the solid blue undercoat.

 Brush twice a week

 Cool to temperate climate

 Semi-long, silky, fine

 Quiet, shy of strangers

DESCRIPTION

Identical to the Russian Blue in its long-legged and long-tailed elegance, the Nebelung has a blue coat, often with silver-tipped hairs on the outer coat. There is sometimes a neck ruff and tufts behind the ears and on the back of the hind legs. Kittens' eyes are at first yellow and turn green in time.

TEMPERAMENT

Nebelungs are quiet cats that usually do not like sharing a home with other pets or children who are loud. They are ideal for older people or families with older children. They are affectionate with their owners, but usually depart when strangers appear.

★ Nebelungs can be very picky about things such as litter cleanliness and food.

More than a century ago, there were longhaired versions of the Russian Blue. In the 1980s breeder Cora Cobb in Colorado bred two longhaired cats and decided to re-create this type. The cat is still rare.

NORWEGIAN FOREST CAT

Brown mackerel tabby and white kitten

A wild-looking animal, the Norwegian Forest Cat emerged from the forest some time during the past 4,000 years. Despite appearances, the coat is easy to care for.

 Very little combing (except for show specimens)

 Can tolerate cold climates

 Long, dense

 Loyal and companionable

DESCRIPTION

The large body is medium length and solidly muscled with substantial bone structure and considerable girth. The large, almond-shaped eyes are expressive and wide set; the outer corner is slightly higher than the inner. The magnificent tail is heavily furred, and remains so even in summer.

TEMPERAMENT

While the Norwegian Forest Cat is an excellent hunter and loves the outdoors, it also craves company. It likes to be handled and petted, and returns this affection in full measure. If a kitten is gently handled and exposed to children, cats and dogs from birth, the temperament will be more adaptable than that of one raised with limited human contact.

★ *The Norwegian Forest Cat will often come down trees head first.*

The water-resistant double coat has a dense, woolly undercoat. Daily combing is recommended when the winter coat is being shed but the cat will normally take care of its own grooming. Surprisingly, its long, thick fur does not mat.

Brown ticked tabby
and white

OCICAT

The spectacular spotted Ocicat has the beauty and athleticism of the wild cat with the disposition of the domestic cat. It is a perfect choice for a family.

Kittens

 Daily hand grooming

 Warm climate only

 Short, tight, smooth

Easily trained and very affectionate

DESCRIPTION

The medium to large Ocicat has a rather long, well-muscled body that is solid and hard. It should look athletic and lithe, not bulky or coarse. The large eyes are almond shaped and are angled slightly up toward the ears. The coat is short, smooth and satiny in texture, with a lustrous shine.

TEMPERAMENT

Because of its Siamese, Abyssinian and American Shorthair ancestors, it exhibits some of the qualities of all three.

It becomes very attached to the people in its family but is not demanding. It does well in a household with other cats or dogs and is usually extroverted and friendly with humans, bright and easily trained.

Blue

★ Although the Ocicat was named for its resemblance to the ocelot, it is not related to it and has no wild blood at all.

The Ocicat comes with small and large spots in an array of eye-catching colors. Very little grooming is necessary, beyond an occasional brushing. Being very sociable, it does not like to be left alone for long periods.

Cinnamon

ORIENTAL LONGHAIR

If you want an elegant-looking, longhaired cat, this one is easier to care for than most—while it has long, silky hair, it has no thick undercoat so requires only moderate grooming.

 Moderate grooming

 Cool to temperate climate

 Medium-long

 Lively, affectionate, show-off

DESCRIPTION

The long, lean Oriental Longhair has a moderate-sized head with large ears. It has a plumed tail. The medium-length, silky coat lies flat and comes in a range of colors, from cinnamon to various tortie tabby patterns. The eyes are green, except for white cats, which have blue eyes.

TEMPERAMENT

These cats are lively and curious, and love company and playing with toys, especially if their owners are attached. They mix well with children and other pets. If you will be leaving your Oriental Longhair for long periods, you should have another cat to keep it company.

★ Cuckoo, the first Oriental Longhair, was a cinnamon color. Today the breed comes in an extensive range of colors and patterns.

In the 1960s, British breeder Maureen Silson bred a sorrel Abyssinian and a seal point Siamese. The result was a longhaired, cinnamon colored cat, which until 2002 was called the British Angora. Its name was changed to Oriental Longhair to avoid confusion with the unrelated Turkish Angora.

Brown ticked tabby

Black and white bicolor

ORIENTAL SHORTHAIR

Oriental Shorthairs run the gamut of colors and patterns. Their sleek lines, intelligence and extroverted personalities come largely from the Siamese from which they were bred.

 Occasional combing for shorthairs; more frequent combing for longhairs

 Warm climate

 Short, fine, close-lying

 Active, playful and loving

White longhair

DESCRIPTION

The body, like that of the Siamese, is sleek, slender and refined. The head is a long, tapering wedge, starting at the nose and flaring out in straight lines to the tips of the ears to form a triangle. The almond-shaped eyes are medium size and slant upward from the nose, following the line of the head and ears. Orientals come in many patterns and more than 300 colors—solid, tabby and spotted.

TEMPERAMENT

Oriental cats are intelligent and love company. They dislike being left alone and can be mischievous if bored and lonely. They will do anything to get your attention and remain playful, high-spirited and affectionate well into maturity.

> ★ *Your Oriental Shorthair will be happier if you monitor its weight and body condition and adjust feeding amounts accordingly.*

Ebony ticked tabby

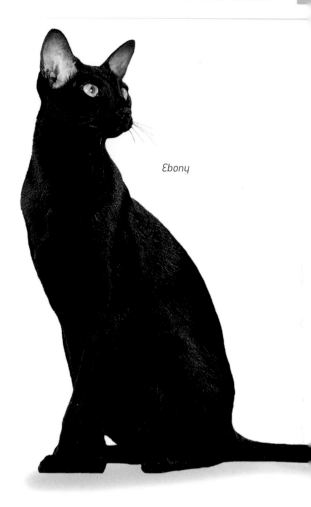

Ebony

The Oriental comes in both shorthair and longhair varieties. The short, fine coat of the Shorthair is glossy and lies close to body. An occasional combing to remove dead hair and a wipe over with a damp chamois to make the coat gleam are all that are needed by way of grooming.

275

PERSIAN

The Persian is prized for its luxurious flowing coat, pretty little face and sweet personality. It now comes in a wide array of patterns and colors.

Thorough daily combing, brushing is essential

Can tolerate cool climate

Double coat, very long, dense, thick, lively

Loving companions, calm, gentle, relatively quiet

Black smoke

DESCRIPTION

The ideal Persian is a medium to large cat with a broad, stocky body and well-rounded head. The cheeks are full and the nose is short, snub and broad. The eyes are large and round, set level and far apart; they should be cleaned daily as part of the grooming routine. The thick coat can be up to 6 inches (15 cm) long, and is soft and dense. The main drawback is that the coat must be groomed every day because it sheds year-round and the cat will have problems with matting and hairballs if the dead hair is not removed regularly.

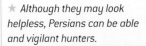

★ *Although they may look helpless, Persians can be able and vigilant hunters.*

This cat became known in Europe in the 1600s. They were originally called Longhairs and still go by this name in Britain. Today's U.S. Persians came about from matings between Angora and Maine Coon cats.

Cream

Chinchilla silver

Show Persians were originally in a restricted color range but today's cats are much more varied, not only in color but also in build, length of coat and face shape. The yardstick for showing, however, remains the blue Persian, first shown in London in 1871.

PERSIAN
CONTINUED

Calm and gentle, the Persian is a lovable and appealing animal. It is hard to resist that little face, almost lost in fur, and fortunately, this cat enjoys being admired, petted and pampered.

TEMPERAMENT

It will pose, draping itself on a windowsill or chair almost like a piece of art. It has a quiet, melodious voice and responds to stroking with delighted little chirps and murmurs. The large eyes are also most expressive of contentment. The Persian enjoys company but is not demanding in this respect and is quite capable of entertaining itself while you are out of the house for a few hours without tearing the place apart. It has a quality of great stillness and serenity and will sometimes sit for long periods doing absolutely nothing except looking beautiful.

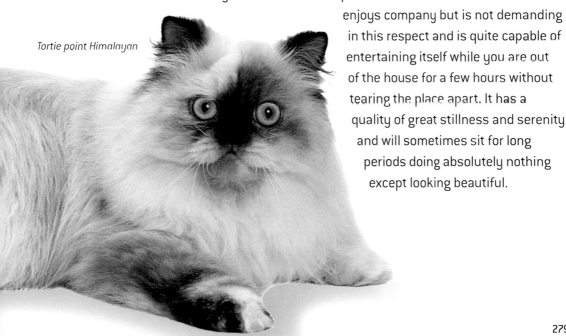

Tortie point Himalayan

RAGDOLL

Blue mitted

The Ragdoll is so named because of its ability to relax totally when handled. This, along with its even temperament and devotion, makes it a good family pet.

 Daily combing and brushing

 Can cope with a cool climate

Semi-long to long, plush

 Affectionate, gentle and tolerant

DESCRIPTION

The ideal Ragdoll has a large, muscular and substantial body. It is massive across the shoulders and chest, and heavy in the hindquarters. The eyes are sapphire blue, large and oval, and the tail is long, fluffy and in proportion to body length. The plush, silky coat is medium-long to long, being longest around the neck and outer edges of the face. Although the fur is non-matting, the coat must be combed daily to remove tangles and dead hair, then brushed gently with a long-bristled brush.

TEMPERAMENT

Known for its loving and adaptable nature, the Ragdoll quickly becomes attached to its owner. It is gentle, intelligent and even-tempered.

> ★ The Ragdoll's color, as with all colorpointed cats, is not fully developed until it is about two years old. The cat continues to grow until it is four years old.

The Ragdoll was developed in California in the 1960s from a white longhair and a seal point Birman. Subsequently, Burmese was added to the mix. It is not recognized in all countries as a championship breed.

Seal mitted

RUSSIAN BLUE

Handsome, gentle and sweet natured, the Russian Blue is in every way a classic. Its elegant lines, rich coat and striking green eyes always turn heads.

 Daily hand grooming

 Can tolerate cool climate

 Short, dense, plush

 Undemanding, intelligent and affectionate

★ *The Russian emperor Czar Nicholas II doted on his pet Russian Blue called Vashka.*

DESCRIPTION

The lithe and graceful Russian Blue has a fine-boned body with rounded, vivid green eyes and wide-set ears that are rather large and broad at the base. Its long, fine-boned legs have paws that are small and slightly rounded, with pads of lavender pink or mauve in the U.S. and blue in Britain. The double coat is short, dense and plush, like seal fur. No other cat has a coat quite like that of the Russian Blue—it has a distinctive soft and silky feel.

TEMPERAMENT

Docile and affectionate, the Russian Blue quickly becomes devoted to its owners. It is gentle, playful and a good companion. Although somewhat shy, it gets along well with children and other pets. It is intelligent, with a quiet, almost musical little voice.

This breed seems to have originated in the most northerly regions of Russia and Scandinavia, and went by a number of names, including Archangel cats, Foreign blues, Spanish cats and Maltese cats. The Maltese label persisted in the United States until the early 20th century.

SCOTTISH FOLD

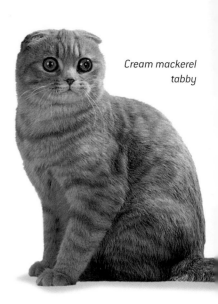

Cream mackerel tabby

The unusual ears of this gentle and affectionate cat can give it the inquiring and puzzled look of a barn owl. It comes in a charming variety of colors and patterns.

 Daily grooming

 Can tolerate a cool climate

 Dense, plush

 Quietly affectionate and well adjusted

DESCRIPTION

The stocky, medium-sized body is rounded and well padded. The large eyes are wide open with a sweet expression. Its ears are this cat's distinguishing feature and should fold forward and downward and sit like a cap on the rounded head. The coat comes in both long and shorthaired versions and should be dense and resilient. Regular brushing will remove dead hair and keep the coat in good condition.

TEMPERAMENT

With its mixture of British and American Shorthair ancestors, the Fold has the best traits of both breeds. It thrives on human companionship, is placid and affectionate, and easily adjusts to other pets. A hardy cat with a sweet disposition, it has a tiny voice.

> ★ *The Scottish Folds are no more prone to ear infections than cats with conventional ears.*

*The first Fold—a white cat named Suzie—
was discovered in a litter of farm cats in
the Tayside region of Scotland in 1961.
All today's Folds are Suzie's descendants.
It has championship status with the Cat
Association of Britain and was granted
championship status in the U.S. in 1978.*

Calico

SELKIRK REX

A well-proportioned cat, the Selkirk Rex is being developed from a spontaneous genetic mutation. As yet, this good-natured cat is little known outside the United States.

Light regular combing

Can tolerate cool weather

Medium-long, soft, plush

Sturdy and affectionate, extremely patient

DESCRIPTION

The Selkirk Rex is a large, heavy-boned cat, rather like the British Shorthair. The eyes are large, rounded and set well apart. Its coat is considerably longer than the other Rex breeds and is soft, plush and obviously curly, with the soft feel of lambs wool. The hair is arranged in loose, individual curls that may be more evident on the neck, around the tail and on the belly. Comb the coat every few days with a wide-toothed comb to remove dead hair.

TEMPERAMENT

Healthy, sturdy and incredibly patient, the Selkirk Rex has a loving, tolerant disposition. It makes a good family pet, although it may be hard to come by as it is a relatively new breed and is unknown in many countries.

★ Selkirk Rex kittens lose their first curly coat. After it has been shed, coarse hair grows sparsely, eventually being replaced by the fully developed adult coat when they are about ten months old.

Brown tabby longhair

The Selkirk Rex originated in Montana, United States, in 1987, in a litter born to a rescued cat. She was named Miss DePesto and bred to a black Persian, producing three Selkirk Rex and three straight-haired kittens. All Selkirk Rex trace their ancestry back to Miss DePesto.

Red classic tabby shorthair

SIAMESE

The Siamese cat is a true aristocrat, with elegant lines and beautiful coloring. It can be rowdy and boisterous, and it is perhaps this contradiction that makes this breed so popular.

 Grooming twice a week

 Needs warm climate

 Short, fine, close-lying

 Inquisitive, mischievous and energetic

★ All Siamese are pure cream or white at birth. The colorpoints on the face, ears, tail, feet and legs appear as the kittens mature.

DESCRIPTION

The ideal Siamese is sleek, slender and refined in every respect, with a long, tapering wedge-shaped head. Its almond-shaped eyes are medium sized and slant upward from the nose, following the line of the head and ears. They are always brilliant sapphire blue; show cats are judged partly by the depth and vivid shades of their eyes. Siamese ears are large, pointed and open at the base. The legs are long and slim with dainty, small, oval paws. The long, thin tail tapers to a fine point and has no kinks.

Blue point

The Siamese coat is short, fine and glossy, and lies close to the body. It can look as if it is "painted on." Grooming is minimal. Combing and brushing twice a week to remove dead hair will be quite sufficient. To make the coat gleam, wipe it over with a damp chamois.

Red point

Seal point kitten

Chocolate point kitten

SIAMESE
CONTINUED

Siamese are colorpoint cats—they have a creamy base coat
with darker shadings on their face, ears, paws, lower legs and tail.
They tend to darken with age.

The original Siamese cats, which still occur in Thailand, bear no resemblance to today's graceful cats—they are stocky with rounded heads and kinked tails. Exclusive to the royal family, they were protected within temple and palace walls and given as gifts to visiting dignitaries.

VARIETIES

Although pure cream or white at birth, kittens develop visible points, or colors, in the first few months of life. Originally, most Siamese had seal (dark brown) points, but occasionally kittens were born with blue (cool gray), chocolate (lighter brown) or lilac (warm gray) points. These colors were initially thought to be inferior and were not qualified for showing or breeding. In time, however, all these variations were accepted by the breed associations and became more common through breeding programs specifically aimed at producing these newer colors. Later, outcrosses with other breeds developed Siamese-mix cats with points in other colors.

Siamese have been crossed with other breeds to create many of today's recognized breeds, including the Orientals, Tonkinese, Ocicat, Snowshoe and Balinese, or longhaired Siamese. The Burmese is descended from a specific cat, "Wong Mau," who was found in Burma in 1930 and bred with Siamese.

Blue lynx point

SIAMESE
CONTINUED

The Siamese is intelligent and lovable. It will continually amuse you with its antics while occasionally frustrating you with its ability to open seemingly locked cupboards and doors.

TEMPERAMENT

It is a people cat and demands attention—the Siamese hates to be ignored or left by itself, and can be mischievous if bored or lonely. These cats communicate like no other. The voice of the Siamese is legendary—a female in season sounds exactly like a baby wailing for its mother and can be easily heard a block away. One of the more highly strung breeds, agile and active and seeming to be in perpetual motion, it is not the cat for everyone. But for those who take this boisterous cat into their home, the reward is boundless affection and hours of entertainment.

Lilac point

SIBERIAN

A magnificent, wild-looking cat, the Siberian is well adapted to surviving in extreme temperatures. Little is known of its background, but some think it is one of the earliest longhaired breeds.

Light regular grooming

Can tolerate cool climate

Long, dense, thick

Hardy and loving companions

Cream mackerel tabby

DESCRIPTION

A large, strong cat, the Siberian differs from the Maine Coon and Norwegian Forest cats in that the general impression is one of roundness and circles rather than wedges and angles. The mature body has an overall sausage shape with tight muscles and large bones. The double coat is moderately long, with a dense, paler undercoat and full ruff. The thick coat protects the cat from extremes of cold in its native land and the oily guard hairs make it water resistant and able to shed snow.

TEMPERAMENT

The Siberian has a sweet personality to go with the sweet expression on its face. It is robust, and makes a loving, gentle and faithful companion.

★ *The Siberian is Russia's native cat. It has been bred there for more than 1,000 years.*

Siberian cats are not common outside Russia but are an ancient breed in their homeland. The coat does not mat, but light, regular grooming is recommended, especially during spring and summer, when the heavy winter coat is shed. This will help to prevent hairballs.

Cream tabby

Brown tabby

SINGAPURA

Small and beautifully proportioned, the Singapura is an extremely pretty cat that enjoys wide appeal. It comes only in shorthair and only in sepia, with ticked fur.

 Occasional combing

 Needs a warm climate

 Very short, fine

 Affectionate and playful

DESCRIPTION

This small cat has a delicate coloring unlike any other breed. It has a moderately stocky, muscular body. The large, almond-shaped eyes are held wide open and are outlined with dark brown. The sleek, silky coat feels like satin. It is fine, very short, and lies close to the body. It needs little grooming beyond an occasional combing.

TEMPERAMENT

Active, curious and quietly affectionate, the Singapura loves to be with people. It remains playful and interactive even when fully grown and gets along remarkably well with other animals. It is a speedy and effective hunter and the queens are noted for being particularly maternal and loving.

★ *The Singapura is the smallest of all the cat breeds. Its name is Malaysian for Singapore.*

The sepia coat color is unique. The ground color is old ivory, with each hair on the back, top of the head and flanks ticked with at least two bands of a deep brown separated by bands of warm old ivory (this is also known as agouti ticking). The underside of the body is a lighter shade, like unbleached muslin.

SNOWSHOE

While comparatively rare, this hybrid of the Siamese and the bicolor American Shorthair has all the good points of its forebears. It is lively, affectionate and very responsive.

 Occasional combing

 Warm climate

 Short–medium, coarse

 Active, playful, outgoing and affectionate

Seal point

DESCRIPTION

The Snowshoe combines the heftiness of its American Shorthair ancestors with the body length of its oriental forebears. With a powerful and heavily built body, it has an athletic appearance of great power and agility, like a runner. The large, round eyes are a vivid blue and the ears are slightly rounded at the tips.

TEMPERAMENT

Lively and adaptable, the Snowshoe combines the best characteristics of its American Shorthair, Birman and Siamese ancestors, and is an excellent hunter. It is full of fun, a good companion and gets along well with other animals. It becomes quite devoted to its owner.

★ The Snowshoe is quite a vocal cat, although its voice is softer than that of its Siamese ancestors.

The glossy coat is short to medium length—the ideal pattern, which is quite a challenge to produce, calls for a solid color on the back and sides with white confined to the insides of the legs and belly. Only minimal grooming is required—an occasional combing to remove dead hair will suffice.

Blue point

SOMALI

Ruddy

With its beautiful coat of many colors, the agile Somali is enjoying a roller-coaster ride to fame and popularity. It makes a delightful and entertaining pet.

 Daily brushing

 Can tolerate cool weather

 Semi-long, dense

 Playful, active and needs human companionship

DESCRIPTION

The medium-long body is lithe and graceful, with strong, well-developed muscles. The almond-shaped eyes are large, brilliant and expressive, gold, green or hazel. They are accented by dark lids and above each eye is a short, dark vertical stroke. Somalis come in red, ruddy, blue and fawn. The hair is ticked.

TEMPERAMENT

Intelligent, extroverted and very sociable, the Somali has a zest for life, loves to play and thrives on companionship. It likes to spend time outdoors and may be restless if confined. It has a soft voice, but is not usually very vocal.

> ★ *The name Somali was chosen for this cat because of its close relationship to the Abyssinian. Somalia and Abyssinia (present-day Ethiopia) are next-door neighbors.*

This longhaired version of the Abyssinian was developed from kittens that carried the longhaired gene. The double, medium-length coat is very soft, extremely fine and the denser the better. It docs not mat, but should be combed regularly to remove dead hair.

Fawn

SPHYNX

Brown mackerel torbie

There are no in-betweens with this cat—because of its appearance, people either love it or hate it. One thing not in dispute, however, is that the Sphynx is the most unusual of cats.

 Daily sponging

 Warm climates; cannot tolerate exposure to direct sunlight

 Extremely short, fine

 Playful and affectionate

DESCRIPTION

The body is sturdy and the large eyes are deep-set. The ears are very large and wide at the base. Despite appearances, the Sphynx is not really hairless. The skin is covered with short, fine down—it feels rather like soft suede. The skin often has a wrinkled appearance, especially in kittens. Because these cats sweat, they should be sponged over daily to remove oils.

TEMPERAMENT

The Sphynx exudes quiet contentment. It has a surprising, mystical effect on anyone holding it for the first time, almost as if it casts a spell over the person. Owners claim that it is the most intelligent and affectionate of breeds.

★ The Sphynx must always be protected against sunburn, as the coat is not substantial enough to screen out the sun's harmful rays.

Black and white kittens

Brown mackerel tabby

In the early 1900s, a cat resembling the modern Sphynx was exhibited as the New Mexican Hairless cat. It was not easily accepted as a championship breed because of concerns that it may have genetic problems. The Sphynx is rarely seen outside the United States.

Black

TONKINESE

Beautiful colors characterize the coat of the Tonkinese, a cat with some of the best qualities of its parent breeds. The result of clever breeding, this cat certainly justifies the effort.

 Occasional combing

 Needs warm climate

 Medium-short, fine

 Inquisitive, active, loving and responsive

Platinum mink

DESCRIPTION

The ideal body shape is between the Siamese and Burmese—medium in size with well-developed muscles. The almond-shaped eyes slant up along the cheekbones toward the outer edges of the ears. Their striking aquamarine to turquoise color is a characteristic of the Tonkinese breed and is the result of combining the blue of the Siamese with the gold of the Burmese. The ears are covered with short hair, and are broad at the base with oval tips. The legs are fairly slim and in proportion in length to the body. The long tail tapers to a slender tip and should have no kinks.

 The Tonkinese doesn't always breed true. Only about half of the kittens of two Tonkinese parents will be true to type, which is the reason it is not accepted by some British associations.

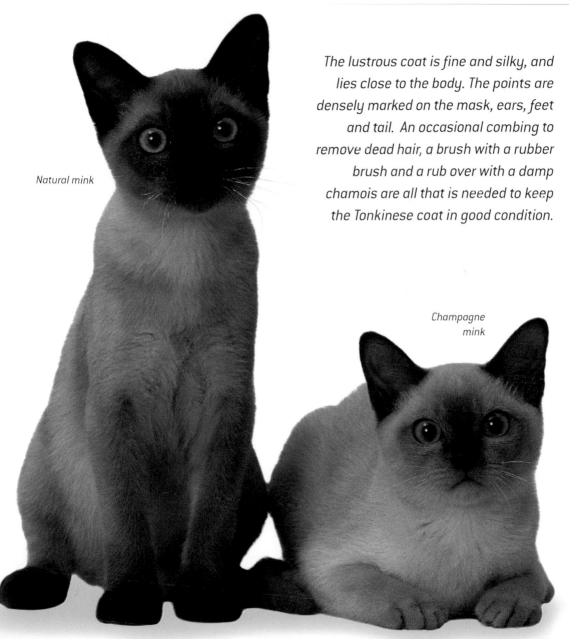

Natural mink

The lustrous coat is fine and silky, and lies close to the body. The points are densely marked on the mask, ears, feet and tail. An occasional combing to remove dead hair, a brush with a rubber brush and a rub over with a damp chamois are all that is needed to keep the Tonkinese coat in good condition.

Champagne mink

The only breed to come out of Canada, the Tonkinese was developed to create a more robust and less stylized form of Siamese. Not all national breed associations have accepted this breed for showing; it was accepted in the U.S. in 1972.

Champagne mink

TONKINESE
CONTINUED

The Tonkinese was developed in Canada in the 1960s by crossing a seal point Siamese and a sable Burmese. In many ways, it is an old-fashioned type of Siamese.

TEMPERAMENT

Intelligent, lively and lovable, the Tonkinese is in every way a charmer, with the strong personality and curiosity of the Siamese evident. It dislikes being left alone for long periods of time and can be mischievous if bored or lonely. If you must be absent for hours at a time, consider acquiring two cats so they can keep each other company. Make sure your home is escape-proof before you bring your Tonkinese home, as it is adept at finding ways to get out. It is playful, affectionate, healthy, long-lived and easy to look after—what more could you ask?

Blue mink

TURKISH ANGORA

The Turkish Angora can truly be called a Turkish delight.
One of the oldest longhaired breeds, strenuous efforts are
being made in its homeland to maintain its bloodlines.

 Regular combing

 Tolerates cool weather

 Semi-long, dense, fine

 Lively, friendly and playful

DESCRIPTION

The ideal Turkish Angora is a lithe, graceful animal with a muscular, medium-sized body. The torso is long and slender and the shoulders are the same width as the hips. The large, almond-shaped eyes slant slightly upward and have an open expression. The silky, medium-length coat shimmers with every movement. It is not fully developed until the cat is about two years old. The hair is mainly straight, but wavy on the stomach. There is a long ruff, with longer hair under the body than on the back.

TEMPERAMENT

Turkish Angoras make wonderful pets and are thought to be among the most intelligent of cat breeds. They are gentle and friendly, with great charm and personality.

★ *White Angoras with odd-colored eyes may be deaf in the ear that is on the same side as the blue eye.*

Silver patched tabby and white

The coat should be combed regularly with a medium-toothed comb to remove dead hair and prevent matting. In order to avoid hairballs, grooming is very important during the spring when the winter coat is being shed.

Red classic tabby

TURKISH VAN

Tortie and white

The most unusual characteristic of the Turkish Van is that it has no reluctance to enter the water. It may have become so adapted because of a need to catch fish.

 Regular grooming

 Can tolerate cool climate

 Semi-long, soft, silky

 Agile, alert and companionable

DESCRIPTION

The Van is a solidly built cat with a broad chest. Its strength and power are apparent in its thickset body and legs. The coat has a texture like cashmere, soft to the roots with no trace of undercoat. It dries quickly after the cat has been for a swim. Combing twice a week to remove dead hair will keep the coat looking good, but give it extra attention when the winter coat is being shed to avoid hairballs.

TEMPERAMENT

This cat has a melodious voice, is active and intelligent, and makes a lively companion to the right owner. It is not a lap cat and will feel more secure, and handle better, with all four feet on a solid surface.

★ *The aggressive nature of the Turkish Van has been tamed successfully by selective breeding. It is now quite a friendly animal but is not a lap cat.*

The Turkish Van comes in only one color—white—and in only one pattern—van. This means that only the head and tail can be colored, and there can be no more than two spots on its body. The origins of the breed were two kittens taken from the Lake Van district of Turkey to Britain in 1955.

Calico

GLOSSARY

altered a cat that has had its reproductive organs removed (either spayed females or neutered males).

banding distinct bands of color in a cross-wise direction.

bib the part of the ruff, or lengthened hair, around the chest area.

bicolor a cat with more than two spots of color on the torso, either white and one basic color, or white with one tabby color.

blaze a marking down the forehead, nose and under the chin.

britches long hairs on the back of the hind legs which run from the hips to the hock, or lower joint, of the leg.

calico van a white cat with two spots on the torso in two different basic colors.

cattery the place where a breeding cat is kept, either in the home or in a separate outbuilding.

cobby sturdy, round and compact body shape. The body is usually set low on the legs, with broad shoulders and rump.

colorpoint a cat with darker shadings on its mask, ears, paws and tail.

double coat a coat of double thickness. Unlike regular coats, the skin is not visible when the coat is parted.

feral cat an untamed domestic cat that was born, or has reverted to living in the wild.

flanks the fleshy sides of the cat between the ribs and the hips.

gene part of the chromosome from which hereditary traits are determined.

ground color the basic (or lighter) color of the cat in any of the tabby patterns.

guard hairs stiff, long, coarse, protective hairs that form a cat's outer coat.

hand grooming light stroking of the coat with your hand to remove dead hair.

in season period of time when the female, or queen, is willing to mate with the male, or studcat. Also referred to as estrus or "in heat."

inoculation the injection of a vaccine to create immunity. A small amount of a specific disease agent is injected enabling antibodies to build up to prevent the occurrence of the disease.

mackerel a type of tabby pattern where the colors of the coat appear striped.

mask the darker shadings on the face.

mixed-breed a cat comprised of two or more different breeds, which do not combine to make a separate breed; not purebred.

mutation a variation in a genetic characteristic which is passed on to following generations. It is either accidental or environmental and can be either harmless or defective.

muzzle the jaws and mouth.

necklace bandings of color across the lower neck and chest area, as if the cat is actually wearing a necklace.

neuter to surgically remove the testicles of a male cat to prevent reproduction.

odd-eyed having different colored eyes, usually one eye is blue and the other is copper or yellow.

particolor comprising two colors, always white with one other basic color.

points extremities of the body comprising the mask, ears, legs and tail.

queen an unaltered female cat.

ruff protruding or lengthened hair around the neck and chest.

spay to surgically remove the uterus and ovaries of a female cat to prevent reproduction.

standards guidelines set out for each breed by all associations which list the qualities that the breed will be judged on in the show ring.

tabby patterned coat with circular, striped or blotchy markings.

ticked dark and light colors on the hair shaft, in alternate bands.

torbie a combination of the tortoiseshell and the tabby pattern that is also known by the name "patched tabby."

tortie abbreviation of tortoiseshell.

tortoiseshell a patched or mottled pattern that can resemble some turtles and tortoises.

unaltered an intact male or female with full reproductive abilities.

van having one or two spots on the torso. The spots are one of the basic colors.

INDEX

S

T

ACKNOWLEDGMENTS

All maps and illustrations © Weldon Owen Pty Ltd. All photographs © istockphoto.com, except 56 br, 77, 109, 165, 176 bl, 185 Getty Images; 111, 164 br Andrew Cummings; 187 Leigh Hyland/RSPCA